THE NEW
AMERICANS

THE NEW AMERICANS

Portraits of an Italian-American Family

Louis J. Palazzi, Jr.

AVVENTURA PRESS

The New Americans

I Nuovi Americani

"The past is never dead. It's not even past." — William Faulkner

©2020 Louis Palazzi

Dedication

To my children, nieces and nephews, and future grandchildren so they never forget our humble origins

Acknowledgements

I would like to thank yy history teachers—

High school Mr. Joseph Festa,

Ithaca College Dr. W. Brown, Dr. R. Ryan, and especially

Dr. Joseph Tempesta

Part 1

Introduction

The media and popular press, led by Tom Brokaw, have extolled the virtues of the past generation of Americans. These people, now elderly, have been given the name "The Greatest Generation" because they were able to create a modern American society from the two catastrophic events of the last century, the Great Depression and World War II. They certainly deserve all the accolades and attention they have received because their achievements were imperative in establishing the modern western world. They came from all over America to serve their country in time of great need. Most of them were the sons and daughters of an earlier generation of Americans who also had to undergo great trials and sacrifices. Their story was one completely different from their offspring's because the majority of them had their origin in a foreign land. They now have all passed away, and with most of them, the stories, perspectives of time and events, and history of what they had to endure to become Americans. The last one in the author's family, Rosa Uguccioni Palazzi, died in 1985 at the very old age of almost ninety-five. This work will focus on the generation of U.S. citizens who were immigrants of the New Immigration, 1880-1920, and hence the first true New Americans.

Until the author's ancestors came to America, the stock of

the nation's human fabric had been mainly from northern and western Europe, being the tall, fair-haired, and light-skinned English, Scots, Germans, and Irish primarily. They all, with the Irish as an exception, had been Protestant in faith and blended into the native stock relatively seamlessly. The people who arrived from 1880 to 1924 were much smaller, darker people, whose customs, traditions, and experiences were vastly different from the original newcomers and other old immigrants. In every sense of the term "new," they were a breed in a country used to a completely different type of people.

The biggest group of these new Americans was the Italians. There has been a lot of literature published after World War II concerning Italian immigration. Most of this has centered on Italian immigration from Southern Italy. All tend to focus on the extreme poverty of the South in contrast to the wealth of Northern Italy, and the authors cite these economic factors as the reasons why so many came to America. They almost always use a U.S. government statistic that says eighty percent of all Italians who came and their descendants were from the South. These theories about the movement of Italians are not completely valid. Almost all of the members of the author's family and numerous others from the same regions were wrongly classified as being "Southern" Italian rather than their true "Northern" origin. This was done by government officials at Ellis Island, and it is on record there. Secondly, the idea of the North having greater wealth was also not correct. Perhaps small farming families in the Northern regions had an extra chicken or pig compared to the South, but their plots of land, homes, education, level of technology, and other economic factors were only slightly different. The true separation was in the cultural distinctions between them. Northerners considered themselves to be more of a part of a nation and Europe, yet they did not neglect their regional identity. Southerners tended to be more provincial, identifying themselves strongly with a local town or area. This work will attempt to offer a fresh perspective on Italian immigration from a family whose origins were predominantly northern. It will, hopefully, explain the events of their lives, in their views, which are unique and vastly different from today's perspectives.

Part II

Post-Risorgimento Italy

By 1860, after a long struggle, Italy had finally become unified for the first time since ancient Rome. With the addition of the Veneto in 1866 and Rome in 1870, the peninsula had become a unified political entity for the first time in almost 2000 years. The common people were promised and expected a better life after they rid themselves of the foreign yoke. In reality, little land reform, economic progress, or industrialization occurred in the latter part of the 1800s. Successive rotating, ineffective, and corrupt Italian governments did little to improve the lot of the majority of Italians, north or south. Partisan bickering had hampered any real progress in improving the lives of commoners, and the economic/social promise of the Risorgimento remained unfulfilled. It is almost a certainty that the social unrest that happened in Italy after World War I would have occurred much earlier if Italy had not been able to export millions of people to the New World. Even the great patriot, Garibaldi, frustrated by the lack of real social and economic progress, led protests in his old age, especially the incident at Aspromonte. Politics and the lack of effective governmental reforms kept the lot of the peasantry basically in the same position in 1900 that they had been in in 1800.

The Italian government was not solely responsible for the

poverty in the countryside (*contado*). Cultural practices and a severe lack of basic raw materials had complicated matters for centuries. Numerous landowners (*patroni*) controlled available land for agriculture, and those plots that were privately owned were extremely small and could not support many people. Lacking primogeniture, land was simply cut up into smaller parcels over the centuries. Because there was no industrial revolution to provide jobs for the surplus population, the peasants were forced to farm even smaller pieces. The rural population had reached a point in the late 1800s where the tiny plots could no longer support them. Even subsistence agriculture was now barely possible. Disease and famine were everyday threats. Social life was based solely on getting enough daily food, which was meted out in very small portions so everyone could exist.

Besides the difficulty of living and producing on a small parcel of land, the living conditions in their homes were very harsh. They lacked all the modern conveniences of life: electricity, indoor plumbing, washing machines, and heat. Floors were almost always dirt. Louis's grandmother Rose Uguccioni's home in Fano was mainly a one-level dwelling about thirty feet by thirty feet. It had a few side partitions, but was mainly open. This area housed a large family with over twelve children. In order to survive, they rented out each corner of the room to two other families. They were considered "wealthy" because they farmed about two acres of flat, rich land near the river, had tenants, and owned a barn that was the size of most modern American sheds today. The homes of his other grandparents were even smaller, with less land. These conditions made it nearly impossible to subdivide properties even further. The breakups were at their limit; other subdivisions would make it impossible to sustain any life. The surplus population now began to look elsewhere to remedy their desperate situation.

Part III

The Lure of America

It was at this time that news of America began to reach the *campagna*. The word, at first, sparked only a trickle of people leaving. By the 1880s, it had turned into a flood. In some cases, especially in the South, whole villages were depopulated. With extremely limited opportunity, and facing grinding poverty for another generation, many decided to go, providing Italy with an outlet for its possible social unrest. They diligently saved money for the trip and purchased passports and passage—nearly all in steerage—in a nearby town. Most came under their own names (that were often changed), but many, like Louis's great-grandfather Attilio, simply came with someone else's ticket! This practice was not unusual as many people changed their minds, having second thoughts about leaving their ancestral homes; over 60% who came to the U.S. went back.

America was perceived as a place having great opportunity to achieve not only a better life, but also substantial wealth. The idea of extensive opportunity was, in reality, partially true. The ability to attain lots of treasure was marginally correct. The average native American in 1900 lived in a state of poverty not really much better than what was in Europe. The newcomers would be competing with natives for a barely marginal existence. Their perceptions, then, were in stark contrast to the reality that awaited them. Sweatshops, steel mills, mines, and factories were the reality——all for pitifully low wages. The natives, most from families who had recently immigrated themselves, now had to compete with the new arrivals for jobs that could barely support their families. The new immigrants faced hatred and discrimination on a level that they could scarcely have imagined. Relegated to the lowest of jobs, many decided to use their peasant skills from the old country to advance their station in life in the new.

Another popular misconception about Italian immigration is that the majority arrived extremely unskilled and took the lowest-paying jobs in garbage, construction, landscaping, steel mills, auto plants, and mines. The skills they had were not those of a maturing industrial society like America, but rather those of an agricultural-peasant society. In those techniques, they were especially proficient. Great-grandfather Attilio was an expert maker of all types of alcoholic beverages, as well as a great businessman. His brothers, Dante and Angelo, were incredible carpenters. His Grandfather Amedeo possessed tailoring abilities (learned from a Jewish immigrant) that today are a lost art. His Grandfather Augusto was first an iron molder, concrete worker, and mason, and finally the most expert gardener in northeastern Pennsylvania. Rose Palazzi had the best-developed business attributes and always had two flourishing enterprises going at the same time. She died in a very comfortable financial situation and always said that if she had been born a man, she would have died a multi-millionaire.

All of Louis's ancestors did not arrive completely unskilled and ignorant, but they certainly were uneducated. Attilio's education level was unknown, probably nonexistent or rudimentary. Amedeo boasted that he had been able to get to the fourth grade before he had to go to work. Augusto had gone as far as grade three before he had to go out and work to support his family on their tiny plot. He always had an extremely difficult time reading and writing English and his native Italian. Rose's alcoholic father, Fortunato, pulled her, the one with the greatest educational promise, from third grade. She was the best student in the class, and her teacher protested strongly, but her father did not want to spend the money to waste education on a female. She hated him for this and other reasons for the rest of her life. Louis's grandmother, Rose Ceccoli Foglietta, the only one educated in America, quit school at age sixteen to help supervise the family business. They all felt the greatest advantage of life in America was that their children could be educated for free, and if they desired, they could go on to college and achieve the educational levels reserved for the nobles, rich, and upper classes in Italy. Amedeo believed the most important profession was teaching, since those people changed the youth for the future. The educational opportunities that did not exist for them were fully exploited by their children, grandchildren, and great-grandchildren.

Part IV

Chief

The story of the author's great-grandfather, Attilio Ceccoli, is one fraught with tragedy. His life was like an ancient Greek drama, with the upsetting ending in contrast to the joyous pinnacle of his middle age. He was born in 1877, in Gualdo Tadino, near Foligno, in central Italy in the province of Umbria. His distant relations, who did not immigrate, still live there. Information on his parents is scant (his father was named Joseph and mother Antonia), but his two younger brothers (Dante, b. 1879, and Angelo, b. 1882), along with his sister (Giulia, b. 1885), eventually also made their way to America. He was a fairly tall man, around five feet, ten inches, with reddish hair and a ruddy complexion. His extreme generosity and amiable personality hid a temper that was violent when flared and tough to keep under control. He was the first of Louis's family to come to America, around 1895. He got there through France, possibly illegally, or more probably assuming the name and ticket of a fellow *paisano* that got cold feet about coming to the New World. He first settled in Jessup, Pennsylvania, near Scranton, working as a laborer and then as a miner. He began to sell wine, beer, and spirits as a part-time business, and in about two years, he began operating his own alcohol manufacturing business at 306 Broadway Ave. in West Scranton. He acquired his expertise in spirits while growing up in Italy. His two brothers, Dante and Angelo, joined him in West Side in 1897. Unlike Attilio, they drank alcohol, but had no skill in making it, and Attilio had none of the expert carpentry skills that they had. In 1899, Attilio, age twenty-three, married Maria Bianca, age fourteen, from Naples. They quickly established a large family, beginning with the birth of the author's grandmother, Rose, in 1900. The family eventually had ten surviving children, but Maria had numerous stillbirths and miscarriages between live births. These reproductive problems greatly weakened her and helped to slowly destroy her health. She was an example of the type of immigrant woman that Margaret Sanger campaigned to provide birth control for in the early 1900s. The family had ten offspring starting with Rose in 1900 followed by Jenny, Johnny, Francie, (Attilio) Joe, Carlo, Antonio, Dante, (Dan) Albert, and Tommy. This large brood was called to order every morning by their father's booming voice; they would all run down the stairs in their large home and then stand at attention while he gave them the orders for the day.

Attilio's business grew by leaps and bounds, and by 1905 he was one of the wealthiest men in West Scranton. He was an example to all Italians and other immigrants of how someone could "make it" in the New World. The reputation of his quality spirits spread rapidly. He and his family manufactured everything in the large basement of their home (now vanished). His clients were almost the entire police force of the city, most ministers, all rabbis, the entire Catholic clergy, and eventually all leading politicians in Lackawanna County, including successive mayors. But his biggest clients were Scranton's famous houses of prostitution, especially the notable Anna Rind's cathouse in the South Side. She carried only his products. His spirits were the oil that fueled the raucous coal town that was known everywhere as the city that "never takes in its sidewalks." Bus and trainloads of young males from New York and Philly arrived every Friday and Saturday night after their bars closed to enjoy the Electric City's whores and Attilio's booze. The exceptional quality of his products, his booming voice, and his commanding control over his children and business earned him the nickname, "Chief." No one called him anything else the rest of his life.

By 1910, the home/business had undergone numerous expansions and improvements. Some production was kept in the basement; some was outsourced with Chief checking on it, and a small part was even moved to some of the kids' rooms. Additions and changes were done constantly to improve his enterprises. By 1915, Attilio had become a U.S. citizen; at about the same time he added, in his usual style, one of the largest bars in the area— in his basement. On busy nights, usually after the town's famous vaudeville shows, the bar was packed, requiring eighteen bartenders to serve everyone. With his metropolitan reputation for excellence continuing to grow, the beer garden was always crowded with Scranton's elite businessmen, politicians, and even wealthy WASP family members. Chief served everybody and invited all ethnic groups into his establishment. His income and wealth continued to grow, but his prosperity revealed a great character flaw. He, raised in great poverty, had had nothing while young; now, when he'd finally succeeded beyond his wildest expectations, he spent everything lavishly on himself, his wife, his home and business, and especially his children. He saved absolutely nothing.

In 1916, on her sixteenth birthday, the author's grandmother, Rose, was given a new car by Chief. She remembered it being a Stutz Bearcat. At that time, people would take their teenagers to Lake Scranton, the city's reservoir, to drive the four miles around the lake and teach them how to operate their vehicles. It was also a social and prestigious event as people drove slowly to show off their expensive cars and clothes. Chief drove the car, with Rose in it, to the lake in order to give her instructions on driving and also to show off on how an Italian had made it in America. Louis's grandmother was never very patient, a character trait she got from her volatile father. The lessons did not proceed well, with both arguing. Eventually, she demanded he let her drive, and he finally relinquished control. She immediately drove the car into the lake. People who were driving by issued a barrage of ethnic slurs, as well as strong laughter. Deeply embarrassed, Chief had the vehicle towed back home and had it sold. Rose never drove again, but each child, when he or she reached the proper age to drive, was given a new automobile.

As the family grew up, all helped work in the business, but also found their own identities. Joe and Francie moved to New York City and were involved in sales. Tony became a wrestler and upholsterer, and Johnny became a middleweight boxer. He mined coal during the day and helped in the business as well as fighting on weekends. He was the Pennsylvania middleweight champion for many years and one of the nation's top ten contenders. He had many famous bouts with Ruby Goldstein, who he said was a dirty fighter because he hit below the waist and rabbit punched. Johnny married the family housekeeper, Helen, who was of Polish extraction. They began their own family and vocations, but tried to remain close to Chief and Maria and occasionally help in the business. By the year 1919, Chief's wealth and standing had earned him tremendous respect in both the Italian community and the Scranton area in general as an example of a successful immigrant. He was at the pinnacle of his life, having achieved more than he or his `paisani` in Italy could ever have imagined.

> "I spent my entire life legally making the finest spirits in the U.S., and now the government is forcing me to become a criminal. I've been accused of being in the Mafia and organized crime, but I never have. All I've tried to do is to make a living for my family and myself. How can you outlaw wine? Wine is life." ——*Chief to his daughter Rose, who relayed it to her grandson, Lou Palazzi, Jr. (III)*

The advent of Prohibition hit the Ceccoli family extremely hard when it took full effect in 1920. Initially, business declined sharply, but after the family moved everything underground, its operations not only recovered, but also rose to heights it never could have conceived. The basement bar, with its numerous bartenders and patrons, was now converted to a speakeasy. Chief knew that conditions had now changed, so he adjusted his tactics accordingly. He immediately contacted local law enforcement officials, judges, clergy, and politicians who frequented his establishment. He guaranteed them free weekly deliveries of booze of their choice if they would keep quiet about his operations. He also asked them to tip him off when raids would occur. He got all to agree to this. Every week his truck made its free, high-quality deliveries to the mayor, city council, judges, priests, rabbis, and ministers, as well as its usual runs to all locals for cash. His numerous grandchildren, nattily attired, were used as decoys, sitting on benches in the front and back of the truck with the illegal barrels under them. Most in the city knew this ruse and chuckled at this newcomer's poor attempts at deception. Cops would open the back, see the kids, laugh, and let it go on. The houses of prostitution greatly increased their demands for his products to satisfy their thirsty clients. Business was very good, but the cost of the numerous liquid bribes ate up a large part of the profits.

The police and other locals continually tipped off Chief to their raids, so the "goods" could be stashed away. One time the state of Pennsylvania decided to conduct its own raid. Somehow the Bishop of Scranton found out about what was to happen. Because he loved Attilio's hooch more than any other, this extremely appreciative client warned Chief about the upcoming event, and the stuff was stowed away! In 1930, at one bust, Maria failed to stash one jug of whisky. Jennie, her daughter, grabbed it, threw a pillow over it, jumped down on the couch, and feigned illness when the cops arrived. The police were inquisitive, but let her go and continued to search, finding nothing. The family also had to branch out its business in order to survive. Chief had contacts in upstate New York, and they divided up production. Son Albert had the most difficult job since he had to drive the big truck over Bear Mountain in the Catskills, at night, with his lights out, in order to send and receive booze. Numerous times he was stopped and temporarily jailed by police, but Chief was always able to get him free and avoid jail time.

During Prohibition, the ethnic slurs, discrimination, and prejudice against the Ceccoli family and other Italian-Americans greatly increased. Before, their wealth had insulated them from the basest elements of American life. Now that they were in a constant fight and struggle, even the people they bribed reminded them who they were, where they came from, and what would happen to them if they didn't get their weekly deliveries on a timely basis. This prejudice did not stop Chief from helping others, even from other ethnic groups. Somewhere around 1925, Attilio and Maria unofficially adopted an orphaned street urchin named Jack Kelly. He was a friend of Johnny's and was taken into the home and treated with dignity and respect, like any other family member. He was given all the amenities the family could lavish on an adopted son. Besides taking care of Jack, Chief gave not only booze but also sums of money to the local churches of all faiths. He even helped the poor on the streets of the Bellevue section of West Scranton. His children said he was generous to a fault.

By 1930, the new FBI had begun to get more actively involved in breaking up bootlegging. Before, the lead had been taken by local and state authorities. Now the emphasis was on those who had avoided being "busted," and the goal was to nail every major producer in U.S. cities. Chief was singled out for destruction in Scranton. Local police had told him the FBI was about to enter the scene, and Chief felt that he would attempt to bribe them also. He tried through the local cops and failed. They repeatedly warned him about the Feds, but he refused to believe anyone would come after him since he paid so much in graft. His peasant stubbornness cost him dearly. Time and time again local authorities tipped him off to liquidate soon, but he wouldn't listen. They also told him something that he completely refused to believe. They said a family member was squealing to the Feds about his operation. He completely ignored this and all warnings. Finally, the day before the big bust, he offered the agents, through the local police, anything they wanted: money, spirits—he had even made arrangements for whores— but he found out graft did not work with the Feds and that his adopted son, Jack Kelly, had been the fink. Jack had been contacted by the Feds in 1930 and was promised a job as an FBI agent if he would rat on Chief's operations. After a lot of federal threats, arm-twisting, and money, Jack had agreed, and for over a year provided detailed information on the family business. When news of Jack's treachery reached Attilio, he could not believe someone to whom he had been so good, in actuality treating him like a son, would betray him. When the big bust came, led by Jack and the Feds, Chief was completely devastated.

In 1931, FBI agents aided by local and state police, busted Chief and all of his spirit-making equipment and holdings. All booze, vats, stills, wine and beer kegs, jugs, and taps were destroyed. The police did not stop there. They went room by room through the entire house and chopped up beds, broke lamps, pocketed jewelry and other personal items, ripped off shelves, and did whatever they could to destroy "the wop's" business. The homestead was in complete ruins when they left. Since Chief could never get insurance and didn't believe in it, all was lost. He also had nothing saved to replace what was destroyed. Jack Kelly was made an FBI agent and sent to Chicago to help them break up Capone.

Chief made his first attempt to kill himself by jumping from the third floor of his home. His suicide effort failed, partly because in mid-leap he had second thoughts and grabbed the nearest clothesline, somewhat breaking his descent. His oldest daughter Rose used to say, "Thank God Pa landed on his head, or he would've killed himself." He survived with minor injuries. He was now fifty-four years old and completely broke. He held on to his home for a few more years, then sold it and lived off the proceeds for the rest of his life.

He joined his youngest daughter Jennie and her husband, Ed Zimkowski, at their home on East Mountain. They never had children, so they took him in, and Chief was given his own room and bath in their spacious home. Prohibition ended in 1933.

In 1934, Maria died at age forty-eight. Years of childbearing and numerous miscarriages and stillbirths had severely weakened her condition. The destruction of the business and the uncertain future of the family hastened her demise. Obviously, this was a severe blow to Chief, who would end up living a very long life.

Chief spent the remaining years of his life with Ed and Jenny. He became a very quiet, elderly man who frequently visited his children, grandchildren, and now great-grandchildren. At first he did this by driving, but by the late 1950s, he gave that up and walked long distances from Jenny and Ed's home all over the city. Grandchildren would drive him to the store or butcher shop, and he would spend lavishly on provolone cheese, steaks, candy, or other goodies. In his later years, Chief reverted back to the skills he had learned in Italy as a child. He was an expert sausage maker, having the grandchildren take him to buy pork he would then turn into the finest Italian links. These he carried around Scranton and gave to his grandchildren, along with his fantastic homemade wine. He was always a welcome visitor, who always spoke quietly to his grandchildren when he arrived from a jaunt. To a point, he seemed to be enjoying his old age.

In early 1960, Chief made a few of his weekly visits to his granddaughter, Alcida Foglietta Palazzi, at 132 Crown Avenue in Scranton. He was about eighty-six years old. A few times, after dropping off some sausage and wine, he asked her to drive him home since he said he was too tired to make the return trip back up the mountain. It was at this time that he began to speak quietly about the course of his life and how this might be the time to end it, since he could no longer make his trips around the city. Alcida and her children all believed he was just talking nonsense, and little attention was paid to his words. One hot summer day in July 1960, Chief made a walk down to Crown Avenue, taking his sausage. He then told Alcida and the children that it was hot, he was tired, and he was going to end his life since he was no good to anyone anymore. Alcida told him to wait in the front, and she would get the car and take him home. Alcida and the children went to the side to get the vehicle and pulled around front. Chief was gone. They drove up Crown Avenue, Stafford Avenue, to East Mountain looking for him. When they got home, Alcida called Jenny and told her what had happened. About the same time, they heard loud sirens, fire trucks, and ambulances. They ran outside, looked down the street towards the Harrison Avenue Bridge, and saw a big commotion. Alcida instructed the children to stay put while she walked the block to investigate. About an hour later, she came back in tears, crying over the death of her beloved grandfather. Attilio had left the front of the house, walked in the opposite direction from East Mountain down to the Harrison Avenue Bridge, climbed up, and jumped off. A high cyclone fence was later put in place to prevent jumpers.

Attilio's life had been an American success story as well as a tragedy like those in ancient dramas. He had achieved, beyond his greatest hopes, a fulfilling life in the New World. Much like the Horatio Alger stories of that era, the first part of his life he lived the American Dream, only to see it destroyed by an unjust act of government based upon ethnic prejudice and discrimination. Two years after the bust, Prohibition was repealed; Americans had turned to buying mass-produced spirits that were factory made. Lack of any capital and the circumstances of change did not allow Chief to start anew. His strong, booming, youthful personality changed, and he became a loving, doting grandparent and the only great-grandparent most of the author's family knew. His suicide not only destroyed his life, but also deeply hurt those who had come to love him in his later years.

Part V

Foxy

Amedeo Dominick Foglietta was born on February 10, 1895, in the town of Civitella Casanova, high in the Apennines in the province of Abruzzo in central Italy. His parents were Lucia Maria Diblasie and Arpenio Foglietta. He was from a family of seven children, but only one other, his younger sister Christine, immigrated to America. She, unfortunately, died giving birth in the late 1920s, leaving no heirs; she was buried in Rochester, New York. Amedeo came from a loving family and was extremely close to his siblings, whose descendants still live in Civitella today. His early life was marked by extreme poverty; his father, a day laborer, had a difficult time providing for the family. Their home, now abandoned and in disrepair, was very tiny for nine people. Even though his mother died young and his sisters married early, his family was barely able to survive. Possessing no marketable skills and finding no available employment, at the age of eighteen Amedeo decided to leave for the New World. After saving up over two years for his passage, he walked and hitchhiked from Civitella to the coastline port of Pescara, and then to a larger port for his trip to America. He arrived at Ellis Island in 1913 under the name Domenico. Later he said he used his middle name because he knew they would never get Amedeo spelled correctly. When immigration officials tried to change and simplify the spelling of his name, he insisted on three occasions that they spell it correctly.

Amadeo's immigration record said he was going to Rochester to live with his cousin, Tom Diblasie. Tommy had been in America for about ten years and was a skilled musician and accomplished saxophonist. Because of discrimination against Italians in the entertainment industry, Tom had changed his name to Evans and had gotten a job with Paul Wideman's famous jazz band. He made a decent living as a professional musician. His reddish hair and fair looks helped him fit into the Tom Evans persona. His cousin Amedeo arrived at his home with absolutely no skills or training in any vocation and with an educational level reaching only to the fourth grade.

In a short time, Amedeo heard that local Jewish tailors, who owned numerous shops in Rochester, were training Jewish immigrants in the trade. They were overwhelmed by the need for skilled, competent tailors due to the demand for their services. Amedeo applied and was rejected many times, but kept returning every day re-applying for a position before, finally, the Friedman family got sick of his pestering and let him start as an apprentice tailor. This was very rare since they usually hired only Jews. He quickly picked up the skills of the trade and in a little while was given a large amount of work to do. His trainer, Sheki Friedman, was impressed at how rapidly he picked up the trade, surpassing trainees that had been there much longer. Amedeo was given a full-time job with the Friedmans, making him one of the few Italians in their shop. He then moved out of Tommy's apartment and into a boarding house.

Amedeo's new residence was a large Victorian homestead in Rochester. He had a small room with a bed and shared a bathroom at the end of the hall with twelve other immigrant men from all over Europe. Most were very large Slavic men from Eastern Europe. They all constantly argued over bathroom time; when Amedeo finally got to use it, it was a filthy mess. It was rarely cleaned. The home was run by a huge, rotund, Irish lady who spoke with a heavy brogue and wore her hair in a tight bun. She treated the newcomers with empathy and compassion, but ran the establishment with an iron fist. After his first day of work, Amedeo came home expecting a decent dinner in the Italian tradition of a long, slow meal of many courses. What he got was immigrant culture shock instead. The woman had all the men(about thirty in total) sit down at a large table, then brought out the food. As soon as she placed the food bowls on the table, all thirty lurched forward to grab as much as they could. Some pushed and shoved and cursed. Food was flying, the Irish lady screaming, and in an instant all bowls were emptied. Dinner was completely gone. Amedeo got nothing that first night, except a few crackers given to him by the sympathetic landlady. The next night, he pushed and shoved his way in like the rest and got his warrior's portion against the much larger men. The food, he recalled later, was the worst he ever ate. The woman's favorite dish was beef stew. It contained lots of potatoes, water, flour, butter, and copious amounts of lard. Every meal had bowls of bland boiled potatoes, even if the main dish had them in it. Other meats, fish, and chicken were either boiled or deep-fried——whatever was easier for her. Amedeo learned to eat extremely fast and carried this poor trait with him the rest of his life.

Rochester in 1915 was an immigrant city fraught with danger at every turn from new arrivals and natives. People of different ethnicities from all over Europe competed and fought individually in bars and on the streets with their own, other, and native American groups. Amedeo had to face many challenges besides just making a living. Trying to survive each day in a foreign land much more violent than his home hamlet was a difficult goal. One dark winter night, after working overtime and just getting paid, Amedeo was assaulted. He was walking down the street when he was attacked from behind by a large, desperate black man carrying a knife. The fight lasted a long time as the smaller Amedeo attempted to hold on to both his savings and his life. After Amedeo disarmed his assailant, both men struggled against each other, using their fists. Amedeo succeeded in badly beating and bloodying the very large man, but refused to kill him and left him on the street. When he returned to the boarding house, his landlady told him he was very lucky since previous tenants had been mugged, never to return. He passed by that spot numerous times and never saw the man again; he never had any other incidents after that.

In 1920 Amedeo left Rochester and moved to Scranton, Pennsylvania, because he heard there was a lot of work in that booming anthracite town. He applied for work at many tailor shops and department stores, but was rejected for jobs because he was Italian. He decided to pressure Old Man Samter at Samter's Department Store for a job. He did this because Samter was a Jewish immigrant; Amedeo had been trained by a Jew and had had no previous success with WASP owners, who wouldn't even interview him. He was rejected four times until, on the fifth try, Amedeo convinced Samter to hire him. He told him he must know how hard it was for an Italian immigrant to get a job, since he was a Jewish immigrant himself. Old Man Samter replied that anyone who came back five times to find a job must really want to work, so he Amedeo employment. He worked there for the next forty-eight years— his only employer.

He first lived at 1205 Pittston Avenue in South Scranton, renting an apartment from another Italian immigrant family, the Spalettas, whose sons became famous local doctors. He developed a close lifelong friendship with this family. In 1921, he met and married Rose Ceccoli, the oldest daughter of Attilio and Maria Ceccoli. After marriage, she moved into his apartment with him. On December 12, 1921, his youngest sister from Civitella, Cristine, joined him in his domicile. She was eighteen, the youngest and only other family member to immigrate to America. She was introduced to John DeMaio, a friend of Amedeo's from Rochester, and they were soon married. Cristine, a housewife, became pregnant in 1924 and died from birth complications in 1925—the first family member to perish in the New World. She was buried in Rochester, New York. Amedeo became the only remaining member of his family in America.

Rose became pregnant almost immediately and miscarried a male late in term. The same situation occurred soon after with another miscarriage. Finally, a daughter, Leonarda, was born on

THE NEW AMERICANS

April 20, 1922. A second daughter, Alcida Cristine, followed her on January 6, 1924. Rose had no more children due to her rare medical condition, a womb that never fully developed. She had a few more miscarriages, but no more live births.

In 1923, the family moved from the apartment to rent half of a double at 632 E. Elm Street in East Scranton. The Rohrick family, recent German immigrants, rented the other half. Both families became close friends and completely enjoyed each other's company. They especially savored each other's ethnic delicacies. Their friendship was strong enough to survive a later move to homes the families purchased at opposite ends of the city.

In 1925, Amedeo had saved enough to purchase his own residence at 430 S. Webster Avenue in South Scranton, in an all-Irish neighborhood. Immediately there were a lot of ethnic slurs about the "dagoes," "wops," and "guineas" moving into and ruining the neighborhood. Amedeo's quiet demeanor, good nature, and his offers of help to his neighbors working on their homes soon won them over. The harassment and ethnic slurs eventually stopped. His immaculate care of the home and grounds showed his neighbors that he would maintain and improve his property, adding to the value of theirs.

He was able to buy his home (for about $2,000) by his prudent saving of money. Most other recent immigrants could never afford a home, especially in the relatively short time of slightly more than a year. When Amedeo got his first week's paycheck from Samter's, he went to the First National Bank at the corner of Lackawanna and Penn Avenues to open an account. When he told the teller his intentions, he was directed to the bank president's office. The bank official was from an old WASP Scranton family. He smiled, shook Amedeo's hand, and thanked him for wanting to open an account at his bank. Amedeo pulled out his weekly paycheck of $9.00 and told the banker he wanted to start the savings with $2.00. He said he used $5.00 for rent, $2.00 for food and clothes, and wanted to begin saving $2.00 per week. The WASP banker was stunned. He issued a barrage of profanities and ethnic slurs screaming about "no-good wops and dagoes" and how this was a great insult. He went on to say that most began with at least $100, then sternly told Amedeo to get the hell out and not waste his time. Amedeo calmly, but forcefully, told the official he was not going to leave and demanded the account be opened. After a lot of yelling and arguing, the man finally agreed to Amedeo's wishes. In a little over a year, he had saved enough to put a down payment of $200 on a home, and within ten years had a large amount of money in his savings account. The banker, admiring his courage, thrift, perseverance, and determination, went to him for all his tailoring needs. The two later became close friends.

Amedeo's quiet personality hid a tremendous amount of inner strength and determination and a toughness that revealed itself while he was a young man on the streets of Rochester and in dealing with a Scranton banker. One other incident showed not only his fortitude, but also a hidden intelligence past his fourth-grade education. Amedeo used to walk back and forth from work every day (`fare una passeggiata`), saying it was the best exercise he could get; plus, he really enjoyed it. He walked past the homes on S. Webster Avenue (almost all owned by Irish-Americans) and enjoyed stopping and conversing with his new friends. His quiet, amiable personality, plus his ability to be a good listener made him a favorite among those porch-sitters who wanted to converse. However, one day on his way home from work, a famous local Irish politician, who had had more than a few drinks, stopped Amedeo and said he wanted to talk to him. He first said he couldn't understand how all his fellow Irish liked him so much since everyone knew that "All you goddamn wops are good for is to be criminals, in organized crime, the Mafia, and carry big guns, and none of you are any good." Amedeo angrily replied, "The only difference between the Mafia and you corrupt, bribe-taking politicians is that the Mafia aren't hypocrites, since they carry guns. You guys are as criminal as they are." Extremely upset that an Italian immigrant had bested him in verbal gymnastics, the man stormed away. When his neighbors heard of the incident, they were happy he had put the "shanty" Irish politician in his place. By this time, the Irish in the hard coal region had begun to divide themselves between those who were liberal, wealthier, and forward-thinking (lace curtain), and those who were heavy drinking, poor, and ignorant (shanty) Irish. As the Old Irish in South Scranton were known for saying, "Some of us are still stuck in the patayda (potato) patch." In 1928, after numerous raises and promotions from the Samter family, Amedeo began to hit his stride, becoming shop foreman. Around the same time, Mr. Horowitz, Mr. Samter's son-in-law, gave him the nickname "Foxy." He did this for two reasons: first, because of Amedeo's bright red complexion and second, because everyone who worked there had trouble pronouncing his name. He was known by this nickname for the remainder of his life. All who knew him used it except his wife Rose, who insisted on the slightly shorter "Amede."

When the Great Depression began in 1929, Samter's, like all businesses, began to lay off employees. Many lost their jobs, but Foxy kept his because he was such a good tailor, had a great work ethic, and possessed an ability to get along with all people of all races and ethnic backgrounds. During these difficult times, he continued to receive his yearly raises and was loved and respected by all. He was considered indispensable by the store manager, Henry Menn (Menicello) and the Samter-Horowitz families. It was also at this time that Foxy became extremely active in the local garment workers' union, fighting for better working conditions for both male and female tailors. He quickly showed his leadership skills by rising to the position of president. He held this position for over twenty-five years. In every yearly election, he was chosen by a large majority, receiving votes from all ethnic groups. In his capacity as president, Foxy traveled extensively— to Florida, Michigan, California, Atlantic City, and wherever the national union gathered for its yearly business meetings. The famous union organizer and national president, Sidney Hillman, was one of Foxy's closest friends. Together they devised union strategies and made plans to try to improve the lives of working people everywhere.

In 1949, Amedeo purchased a "new" 1948 Packard automobile from a local judge. The barrister had purchased the large, luxurious automobile for his wife. However, even though purple was his wife's favorite color, she decided she did not like it on a Packard car. Knowing that Foxy loved Packards, America's choicest car at that time, the judge called and gave him a great deal because of the unusual color. That was Foxy's most prized possession; it was a great symbol of his success in his adopted land. He used to remark that he never imagined, given the abject poverty of his youth, that he would own such a nice home and America's finest auto. The only thing he valued more than his family, home, and Packard, was his American citizenship, which he treasured.

By 1950, Foxy had risen past shop foreman and now supervised the entire floor of tailors. He had three to five foremen under him and twenty-four tailors, making it the biggest tailoring enterprise in Northeast Pennsylvania. The whole floor hummed with activity, from the whining of sewing machines to the hissing sounds of the steam presses for dress pants. Foxy continued to work on the floor, handling special assignments given to him by the Samters, usually from well-heeled clients. This work he did personally, and it was considered a great honor to have him fit you for a suit. Many large men with unique body builds from athletic to portly sought him out for a fit. He was considered the finest tailor in the city because he handled only the most difficult problems no one else would touch. Satisfied customers would offer him large tips, which he always refused, saying it was his job to always do his best. The clothes he made fit perfectly; his high sense of professional standards would have it no other way.

Foxy wrote many letters to his family in Italy and on many occasions also sent money. In 1950, his only brother, Pasquale, asked him to begin the process of attempting to bring him to the USA. He hired a lawyer to begin drawing up the required documents, but the entire thing did not last long. Even though Foxy was Pasquale's brother, making the process supposedly easier, he was unable to bring him to America. The Quota Acts of the 1920s, still in force, severely discriminated against further Italian immigration. Having an immediate blood relative already in the country should have made entry a given, but it did not work in Pasquale's case. A second attempt was made in 1954, and this also failed. Finally, in 1964, reform legislation was passed and signed by President Johnson, making it more equitable for Italians. Foxy wrote to his brother about these changes, but Pasquale was almost sixty-five by then and decided to stay in Civatella.

In 1966, at the age of seventy-one, Foxy retired from Samter's. He had wanted to retire at the age of sixty-five, but the Samter family convinced him to stay, saying they could not operate the shop without him. They gave him a large retirement dinner attended by family, friends, owners, fellow employees, and labor leaders from throughout the USA. Foxy finally "packed it in" after this affair. He spent his retirement time watching TV (especially the Gillette Friday Night Fights), smoking cigars, and helping his son-in-law, Lou Palazzi, Sr., run his garden center. He was a doting, loving, and caring grandparent to his six grandchildren from Leonarda in Harrisburg, Pennsylvania, and his four from Alcida, four blocks away in Scranton. He was an especially fun babysitter, playing cards and checkers indoors, and baseball and football outdoors with his secondary offspring. He showed himself to be one of the few people who completely and absolutely enjoyed every aspect of being retired.

In 1973, about the age of seventy-eight, he began to pass blood in his stool. He was diagnosed with colon cancer. At that time, there were few drugs or treatments for the disease. He lived with his daughter Alcida and family for the next two years while the cancer spread slowly. By 1975, it had destroyed him. He left his wife Rose, who lived another seven years, his two daughters, and ten grandchildren.

Foxy had always told the family that his journey through life was a great American success story. His poverty, humble beginnings, and lack of a vocational skill did not prevent him from having an extremely successful and enjoyable life. He learned a trade from another immigrant and used it for his life's work, which he practiced with the utmost skill and mastery of the vocation. He was an accomplished tailor and a person of tremendous strength and personal ethics. He was a great example to his children and grandchildren. His civil demeanor, coupled with his quiet, amiable personality, won the respect and admiration of all ethnic groups in Scranton. Foxy's profession was tailoring, but he really regretted not being a teacher. He always said that teaching was the most important profession since it influenced and changed the next generation for the future. He never realized that he was also a master educator, showing and leading his family and others by his great personal example.

Part VI

Creator of Beauty

Augusto Palazzi was born on March 26, 1884, in the San Leonardo enclave in Fano, province of the Marches of Ancona, on the Adriatic coast in Northern Italy. His family probably originated from one of the small mountain towns outside of Fano, like Montemaggiore, since he always said he was a "mountain man" and not a true Fanese. The family's beginnings are obscure because of the numerous Palazzis and Palazzinis scattered throughout the hills of Marche. Most of these people eventually made it to North America.

Augusto was the youngest son of Luigi Palazzini and Tombari (Anna or Nina) Fortunata. He had five older brothers: Lavinio, born 1874; Massimo, 1875; Eugenio, 1878; Alipio, 1879, and Attilio, 1881. Only he, Massimo, and Attilio survived to adulthood. The others died between the ages of eight months and eighteen, probably from being malnourished. His parents married late in life; Luigi was thirty-four and Nina over twenty-nine. His father, to differentiate the family from the other numerous Palazzinis in the region, shortened the name to "Palazzi." Other distant relatives also did this. At first, the family lived with the Pasuccis, not being able to afford even a humble home of their own. Then they settled in a tiny, cramped residence in the small section of San Leonardo. Life was tedious and difficult. The limited production of the home/farm, coupled with Luigi's day laboring, barely provided enough for the family. Starvation was always a real threat, and Nina meted out food in small portions. Augusto always complained in later life of how little he had to eat as a child and how he was always hungry. Sumptuous dinners with large amounts of food were a requirement when he later ate in the United States.

Augusto's parents were able to pay for his education up to the third grade. They had to remove him from school after that because they could no longer afford to keep him there. He had to help his family financially by working at odd jobs. He did learn how to do basic math, and he picked up some ability to read and write. His education level was, at best, only rudimentary. Later in life, he had to ask his numerous grandchildren for help in doing bills and in reading important documents. He constantly attempted to improve these skills, but he had limited success. However, during his youth, Augusto did acquire many other peasant attributes, probably at home from his parents. He became an expert winemaker, an accomplished accordion player, and was always meticulous, neat, and perfect in appearance, deportment, and manners. His demeanor and personality later were greatly reflected in his work in the United States when he became a master gardener.

Augusto's lack of education did not leave him without certain abilities. He knew all the peasant avocations of the day. He could make anything grow and bloom profusely. He made and blended white and red wine that was simply extraordinary. His handling of the musical instrument of his youth showed an intelligence and ability far beyond his limited schooling. However, his subsistence agricultural background and the skills he got from that type of life did not fit what was needed in Italy in 1900 or in the United States.

From his birth until 1905, Augusto lived with his family and worked at home as well as laboring in any capacity where he could find employment. In 1898, his mother died at age fifty-four when he was only fourteen. He never talked about her after that. This was the first great shock of his youth and helped to shape his personality forever.

THE NEW AMERICANS

Augusto finally spoke of his mother on his deathbed in 1964, saying that he had just come to know her when she died and left them. He greatly lamented her death. This first blow struck him hard, leaving him despondent and sullen. He carried these traits his entire life.

On December 4, 1898, his older brother, Massimo, married Maria Radi. They then moved to another home nearby in Fano and began a small but prosperous business selling various and sundry items. Augusto and his only other surviving older brother, Attilio, remained at home with Luigi working jobs as they could find them, returning at night with their wages—mere pittances. In 1905, Attilio married Albina Giuliani, and they all lived together in the family homestead with Luigi. In a very short time, Augusto developed an adversarial relationship with Albina. She was a bossy, domineering woman who was as stubborn (*"testa dura"*) as Augusto. He felt she was too demanding and tough on his brother Attilio. The bad blood in the home finally resulted in Augusto's having to leave. Massimo and Maria agreed to let Augusto live with them and their five-year-old daughter, Nina. He moved into their home around 1906 and began to help in their business along with his usual day laboring. His new daily existence with his brother and family was no different from before; it was a struggle to simply get enough to eat on a regular basis. The thought of getting more than simple sustenance took a few years and another addition to the family to develop.

In 1908, two events shaped Augusto's future. His brother's family grew again with the birth of a son, Ugo. The small household now became very crowded, so Augusto decided to go out and find a wife of his own so he could move into his own domicile. He met, dated, and proposed to Rosa Uguccioni, age sixteen (he was now twenty-four), who rejected him to marry a much wealthier middle-class fish merchant, Giuseppe Tomassoni. Augusto, once again, suffered a serious blow to his psyche. Because of the crowded circumstances in his brother's home and the subsequent rejection of his marriage proposal, he decided to embark for America. Returning to his father's home, with his witch of a sister-in-law, Albina, was never considered. Augusto finally began to realize that perhaps life could be better somewhere else. Even though he had no vocation, he thought that America offered a much better opportunity for advancement than Fano.

Augusto was almost twenty-three when he arrived at Ellis Island on March 13, 1908. He was listed as five feet, five inches tall, and wrongly classified as "Southern Italian." He immediately boarded a train for New London, Connecticut to live with his cousin, Ricardo Cannestrari. He went to New England because of a cousin who lived there and also because of the large Fanese/Marchegiano population there. Like all immigrants before and after, he went to a place where his fellow *paisani* from the same town or region clustered. Augusto was no different from the rest. However, he was not the first Palazzi to come to the New World. His great-grandfather, a Palazzini, had come to the U.S. in 1776. He had joined Washington's army in the struggle for American independence. He fought the entire war, returning to Fano in 1783. The musket he purportedly

used in the fight was a prized family heirloom and hung over the fireplace in the old homestead. It is no longer extant.

Augusto immediately found work in a foundry working as an iron molder. He used to say that if you couldn't find work in this country, something was wrong with you. The wages were extremely low, the work very hard, and the hours long. However, it was permanent employment, and almost all his fellow molders were Italians. This was the type of work most Americans refused to do; it was even beneath the other recent immigrant groups. Like the other menial jobs of the day—garbage collecting, street sweeping, gardening, etc.—it was relegated to the lowest unskilled newcomers, the Italians. Augusto used to recollect that it was not a very attractive job, but it was better than nothing, like in Fano.

By 1910, Augusto had been making a steady income; he wrote to his family in Italy, urging them to come to America. On April 27, 1910, his brother, Attilio, arrived, having left his home with Luigi and family in San Leonardo. He was listed at Ellis Island as being five feet, four inches tall, and a farmer. The documents said he was going to New London to live and work with his brother, Augusto.

THE NEW AMERICANS

His wife and sons joined him briefly in America, but soon returned to Italy because of the insults, prejudice, and discrimination against Italians in New London. Augusto's dislike of Albina intensified because she continually urged Attilio to return home. Later in the year, even though he had steady employment at the foundry, Attilio went back to Fano on his wife's orders, despite his younger brother's admonition to stay. Attilio stayed less than a year in Italy and then went back to his brother in America. He found less work in the old country than before, which led him to go back to the only available job for him in the New World. He labored over two years in the cauldron of fire that was foundry work while his wife continually sent pestering letters begging his return. Attilio, unlike his younger brother, was much more sensitive to the constant ethnic slurs, insults, and prejudice that were a daily occurrence. Finally, after some years, he went back to Italy in 1914. Augusto once again warned him about returning because of the lack of opportunity in Fano and the gathering war clouds in Europe. Attilio did not heed his younger brother's advice, and later he suffered tragic consequences. Augusto cursed his brother's wife and forbade any contact with her and her children for eternity. Attilio's existence remained a mystery to Augusto's descendants until 2000, and there was no contact with Attilio's descendants until 2002.

On March 27, 1911, Augusto married Artaserse Spadoni. She was also from the same Fano region as Augusto, but little else is known about her. They had two children: Lena, in 1912, and Libero, in 1914. The marriage was a difficult one from the start as both had difficulty getting along. Augusto also suspected that while he was at work, his wife was having affairs with different immigrant men in New London and Massachusetts. In 1915, while he was at work, Artaserse left with the two children to parts unknown. Augusto searched for them for two years, without any success. The local police did not expend a great deal of effort in attempting to find an immigrant's lost family. A few years earlier, in 1912, Augusto had learned of his father's death. This event, plus the demise of his mother, his brother Attilio's situation, and now his wife's desertion, hurt him greatly. His personality had developed as a shy, quiet individual, and now he carried a withdrawn personality the rest of his life. While his grandchildren were growing up, they would question the weird nature of their grandfather, who was always so despondent and grumpy. Their parents always told them that he had had a lot of "family problems" when he was young. Only after recent research did they learn of the extent of the pain he suffered as a young man. When they had the courage to question him about his first wife, he would respond, "She was a pig." Their parents satisfied their inquisitiveness by saying she was a poor housekeeper. They know now that his meaning had nothing to do with being clean. Unfortunately for him, his family problems were to get much worse before they finally improved. In 1917, Augusto had the Italian consulate in New London draw up divorce and custody papers against his wife. Local police, giving him lip service, said they continued to have no leads on the location of his family. In court on March 22, 1917, his wife failed to appear, and Augusto won custody of the children and a divorce from his spouse. The court papers stated she had committed adultery with William Salvadori numerous times in November of 1915 in Fall River, Massachusetts. In the late 1920s and early 1930s, Augusto made yearly trips to visit relatives in Taunton, Massachusetts, near his old New London haunts. During this time, his niece, Nina Palazzi Alegi, found his ex-spouse and two children. Artaserse allowed him to take Lena and visit with their *cugini,* but she kept young Libero close to her skirt, fearing Augusto would take the child. His life had changed dramatically by this time, and he was content simply seeing his son and daughter. He abandoned any future attempts at custody.

In 1917, Augusto, alone, continued to labor at the foundry. He kept in touch with his older brother Massimo and his family in Fano. Massimo informed Augusto that the Italian army had successfully recruited his thirty-six-year-old brother Attilio. Attilio had to join the army in order to provide for his struggling family. He became a member of the Bersaglieri, (15th Regiment, Second Company), Italy's elite troops. During the fighting in the Alps against the Austro-German armies, he was wounded and taken prisoner. He was put into a POW camp in Kleinmunchen, Germany. Attilio remained there until he died on September 7, 1920. Since most Italian POWS had been repatriated by this time, it was assumed his wounds were so severe that he could not be moved. In 1918, Augusto received word that his forty-three-year-old brother Massimo had contracted the Spanish flu. His condition continued to worsen, and on September 23, 1918, he expired. He left a wife and four children in desperate circumstances. All eventually later made their way to North America. The ill fortune ("`fortuna malata`") of Augusto continued as he tried, one more time, to return to his homeland to find employment. Once again, he was unsuccessful and came back to the New World on June 4, 1920. He went to work at the same vocation reserved solely for immigrant Italians. He now remained as the sole surviving member of his generation of the Palazzi family.

After his fruitless search for work in the old country, he was determined to find another type of job rather than the brutal iron molding. He finally got a job as a gardener working for a wealthy WASP family who were the cousins of the Astors. He rented a room in New London from Enrico (Riccardo) Uguccioni, the brother of his ex-girlfriend, Rosa Uguccioni. After coming home from work one day, he discovered Rose at Enrico's home with her eight-year-old son, Silvano. She and her son had recently immigrated to America and were visiting from Scranton. Rose's matchmaking brothers, believing she and her son would soon be a financial burden to them, quickly pushed the two into marriage. In a very short time, they were betrothed, and in June 1921, another son, Luigi Palazzi, was born in an apartment in Groton, Connecticut. Silvano was very upset at his mother's marriage because he now had a competitor for her attention. He became even more jealous with the birth of his new half-brother. Augusto quickly sensed Silvano's anxiety and decided to bring him a gift to win him over. He asked his employer for an almost new, bright red pony cart that his son didn't like and refused to use. Mr. Plante, his boss, liked Augusto's work ethic and told him to take it home for his stepson. Silvano was filled with joy at getting such an expensive toy. He told his new stepdad that he was the best father a kid could have and that Augusto could bring home the pony to go along with the cart any day he saw appropriate.

LOUIS PALAZZI

The pony never arrived.

Later in 1921, Augusto, Rose, and their family moved to Dunmore, Pennsylvania, and took up residence on Apple Street. He got a job working for Baumann Landscaping full-time and began a part-time gardening business on nights and weekends. He purchased a metal-wheeled wheelbarrow, (which was in the family until 1964), a rake, a pick, and a shovel. He went house to house knocking on doors asking if people needed work done. Besides doing the usual gardening, he also did a lot of masonry work, carpentry, and other odd jobs, doing all that was asked to make money. By 1925, he and Rose had saved enough to get a mortgage to build their own residence/business. The birth of Bruno (Bernie) in 1925 also necessitated a move. Augusto eyed a triangular piece of property at 700 S. Blakely Street that was supposed to become a public park. Many had attempted to buy this, but its nebulous legal status and the borough's intent to make it a public facility ended their inquiries. This did not deter Augusto from trying to get it. He found out from Old Man Mastrianni, who had been in Dunmore a long time and who was a local politico, that it could be purchased. He told Augusto that the council had never officially voted to make it a playground; if Augusto came up with the required cash, he could have it. He also told him he would also arrange a mortgage for him. The cash graft was paid, the mortgage and construction loan arranged, and building began. Since the neighborhood contained primarily WASP, Polish, and Irish families, they were to be the first Italians within three to four blocks. When building began, the neighbors began complaining, using the excuse of the lost park, but in reality they did not want "dagoes" in their ward. When Augusto took an inordinate amount of time in making a perfect wine cellar, it aggravated them greatly. They began to yell and scream at him for his slow pace, the loss of their park, and his absolute refusal to talk to them. When he was able to obtain another small six-foot strip of road to add to the property (thanks to an additional cash gift to Mastrianni), they issued a barrage of profanities and ethnic slurs every time he showed up. When the edifice was nearing completion, Augusto decided to retaliate in a unique, unorthodox fashion. To further incense his new neighbors, he had the entire home covered in bright pink stucco instead of the more conservative colors of the day. He said he had to look at the exterior only on occasion; his fellow non-Italian neighbors had to look all the time.

In 1925, his business became full time. Augusto bought a Model T pickup and adopted the moniker "Creator of Beauty." His slogan reflected his primary occupation, growing plants and caring for them. However, he also did other types of work. Odd jobs, carpentry, and especially some concrete work were also done. He took an inordinate amount of pride in what he did, making sure the entire work and property were neat and clean before he finished. He would do things not part of the contracted services simply because his work wouldn't look right unless something else was also completed. Most times he would be on his hands and knees near the completion of a job, hand cutting the grass edge where it met the bed so his work would be perfect.

"She's a-good or she's a-no good——there's- a- no in-between.""

"You can make-a you life work, or you can make-a you work your life." "

"My work-a, she's a-my advertisement."

These philosophical mottoes were how he ran his business and trade. He preached these on a constant basis. Augusto had one other unique business technique. This was a tradition after every job. He would break out a bottle of his homemade wine and insist that the clients drink it with him while he described his work. He would then tell his reasons for doing it a certain way and would also offer suggestions for the future. This primitive form of customer relations was truly a work of genius, considering his limited business training and education. This tradition, in many forms, is carried on to the present day.

Augusto's thriving business at 700 S. Blakely Street greatly contributed to the family income and status to a degree that had been unobtainable in Fano. His formal, neat, clean gardening style fit with the numerous estates of the wealthy in Scranton and surrounding communities like Clarks Summit and Waverly. He was only heard once admitting defeat to another landscaper, telling his son Lou and grandson Lou, Jr. (III), "I'm-a the best, except for that son-of-a-bitch Frenchman from Stroudsburg, LaBar."

Augusto's forte in gardening was lawn renovation. He did this better than anyone else, and it was the best part of his trade. *"Watch This Grass Grow, A. Palazzi, Landscape Gardener"* was the sign he put out when he redid lawns. He and his crew would first comb the grass with hand garden rakes, completely de-thatching the lawn. Then he and other short Italians, in their green Dickies work clothes, would drag a medieval-looking, water-filled roller with huge spikes across the lawn, making many holes. Augusto would then hand seed the area and apply fertilizer and lime. The final step was his family secret. He would use a special narrow tine rake and rightly drag it north to south and east to west. This process would put a fine amount of soil over the seed. He then would roll it (without water in the roller) and apply clean straw—never hay. The grass always grew at a fantastic rate. A nearby client, Mrs. Genovese, asked him to renovate her lawn. They both agreed on a price, and work began. While he was working, she came out and saw him up a tree, cutting off limbs. She was upset and said to him, "Mr. Palazzi, our agreement was to fix the grass, not to prune the trees." He replied, "If I no cut-a these a-limbs, the grass a-she no grow." She went into the house without comment. He knew the value of sunlight for grass to prosper. On numerous other occasions, work would begin, and clients would come outside and try to tell him what to do because he was a recent immigrant. In some instances he would talk with them and ameliorate the situation, and in others his peasant stubbornness would take over, and he would leave and tell them to get someone else. He always told Jewish-American customers that their price was ten percent higher than he would normally charge. When they told him this was discriminatory and asked why, he always responded that it wasn't prejudice, but a character trait of their ethnicity that made them more demanding than other ethnicities in Northeast Pennsylvania. He always stuck to his quoted price or less, never adding any additional charge except for hauling, which was $5.00.

In 1933, Augusto decided to build an octagonal gazebo/storage shed in his garden center next to his numerous plants. He constructed the building and put a clay-colored terracotta steeple roof on it, similar to the types used in Italy. He could not make up his mind on the siding for his new construction. One day, while he was driving on Lackawanna Avenue in downtown Scranton, he saw stacks of perfectly rectangular pieces of marble, two inches thick, outside of a local bank. He went in and asked the workmen if he could have them. They said the new WASP bank president hated marble wainscoting and wanted it removed. They were to replace it with American walnut. This polished marble, of Italian origin, was discarded outside; they told him to take it so they would not have to haul it away. Augusto, with the help of his sons Tom, Lou, and Bernie, made two or three trips with his pickup to get it all and take it to his Dunmore home. These marble pieces, fastened with special three-inch bronze screws, became the incredible new siding of the gazebo. This marble, coupled with the terracotta roof, made a truly unique structure in Northeast Pennsylvania. Later, Augusto returned with the boys to retrieve all the broken pieces damaged in removal. The workers there, along with his sons, were intrigued at why he would take broken marble of all types and sizes. The tight-lipped Augusto said nothing when they all inquired. One of the workers told the bank president what Augusto and sons were doing while they were in the middle of the task. He came out to look and then exclaimed to them, "You goddamn guineas will take any garbage." With that statement, Tom, now twenty-two, made a beeline for the guy. Augusto quickly instructed Lou and Bernie to get their brother before he killed the bank president. Tom was restrained, and the broken marble, of many various sizes and shapes, was mortared with dark brown cement to become the fabulous floor of the bar in his wife's restaurant, The Gridiron. The marble rectangles on the gazebo have since disintegrated due to the wet climate of Northeast Pennsylvania and were replaced by cedar shakes in the 1970s. The attractive broken pieces that made up the floor in the bar remain today, a testament to the vision of the Creator of Beauty. Even though the Great Depression severely hurt the family business and made life as difficult as it had been in his youth in Italy, Augusto's rudimentary business skills and determination allowed him to avoid the abject poverty suffered by so many other Americans. He was able to keep all that they had worked so hard to achieve. Nothing was lost at this time. The home/businesses, trucks, etc., remained in the family, and business continued to be good, but payment was low and price-haggling common. Their situation was in stark contrast to their other neighbors in Dunmore of both Italian and other extractions who had lost homes, jobs, personal possessions, and especially their self-esteem. This national calamity did create a more level playing field for his three sons to compete against others. No longer were they the lowest. Now everyone was at their level; in most instances, the newcomers were even a little higher. Acceptance of Augusto's children into American life in the 1920s had been difficult; now with different social conditions, it was possible.

In 1943, when Augusto was almost sixty, he decided to move back to New London and work as a printer. His gardening business had slowed during the war, and he was tired of the hard physical labor involved in it. He was adamant about this even though his wife and family strongly opposed the move. Bernie was pulled out of high school in his junior year at Dunmore, and was very upset at being separated from his friends. Lou was graduating from Penn State; he got a job in New London building aircraft carriers. Tom was a physical education teacher and coach in Dunmore, but managed to join the family in the summer working in a grocery store.

Fortunately, the Pennsylvania properties were not sold, because after a year they all returned, Augusto vowing never to work for anyone else again. He told everyone that it was better to be a "pushcart dago" selling vegetables on the street than to work for other people. Like all in the author's family, Augusto believed strongly in becoming an independent businessman putting up with the fickle personalities of homeowners rather than laboring for someone else for meager wages. America provided many opportunities for his ancestors; they chose the course of becoming small entrepreneurs rather than slaving in the mines and mills. This decision enabled them to acquire vastly more wealth than they ever could have gotten had they remained in Italy.

Augusto visited his nieces and nephews on a regular basis from the 1930s until his death in 1964. These were yearly affairs to Taunton, Massachusetts and later to Windsor, Ontario, Canada. He attempted to bring his nephew Federico and his family to Dunmore in the early 1950s, but the restrictive Quota Acts of the 1920s were still in effect and it could not be done. Instead, they settled in Windsor, in Canada. Augusto also made additional trips, by himself, to visit his ex-wife and take his daughter Lena out with him and his nieces. His ex allowed this, but would never let him take Libero, his son. He would talk with him, sit for a while, and then leave. He kept these visits secret from his family in Dunmore so as not to hurt his wife Rose and his sons. Most of the time he accomplished this while going to nurseries in Connecticut to purchase shrubs.

In the late 1940s, Augusto moved his garden center across the street. The old center was made into a gas station, another one of his wife Rose's enterprises. He continued to work but slowed down considerably, taking only those jobs he knew were for credible people who gave him very little grief. He kept very busy, but was finally able to enjoy life— making wine, playing his accordion, and enjoying his growing number of grandchildren, with whom he spent time, but spoke to only a bit. "There's a-time a-to a-talk and a-time a-to shut up, and for a-most a-people they'd a-be better if a-they'd a- shut up and a-do a-more work." He said this many times to his loquacious offspring, especially his female grandchildren who had the most difficult time understanding and speaking to him. Augusto also made many return trips to Italy, the first one being in 1949 with Rose and again in 1954, 1956, 1960, and 1962. He made all the journeys with his wife except the 1956 voyage, which he made by himself to find a special Italian accordion for his grandson, Tommy Silvano, Jr. He returned to his native town and region as a man of substantial means who had succeeded in a foreign land despite the great odds against him, his poverty, and lack of an education. It was especially gratifying for Augusto to be able to afford the trip, eat well, and to dress neatly, wearing the finest clothes.

The Creator of Beauty's quiet demeanor and stubbornness was legendary in the family and surrounding community. He demonstrated this on numerous occasions. He rarely attended his sons' football games, not understanding the sport and believing the great effort required to play the game would be better spent working. He did take great pride in what they had accomplished on the gridiron. When his son Lou played college and pro football and then became an NFL umpire, Augusto did go to a few games. In 1960, after watching an Eagles game that Lou umpired in Philadelphia, his family went to the famous restaurant, Bookbinders, for dinner, taking Rose and Augusto with them. While they were being served, an African-American waiter came over to fill the water glasses. Augusto walked out and refused to come back in. They all wondered what was wrong with him so Lou, Sr. went outside to find out the problem. The others looked out the window to see both arguing; finally, when Lou came in, he told the rest of the family that his father did not want to be served by a black man. He went on to say that when he had come to America, he had learned very quickly that Italians were at the bottom of society, but blacks were beneath them, and he would have nothing to do with anyone inferior to him. He sat outside on a bench while the rest of the family ate. Tom, Lou Sr., and Bernie used to explain his behavior by saying, "Well, you know how Pa is; he's different." In 1962, at Brutico's restaurant in Old Forge, Pennsylvania, the family was eating pizza for dinner, but Augusto had to have pizza made a special way. Instead of mozzarella as a topping, grated locatelli cheese had to be used for his. This, he said, was the type they had eaten in the mountains around Fano. This special request greatly aggravated the owner, Old Man Angelo Brutico, who always made a point to tell him what a problem it was to make it this way. They both argued every time the family ate there, and had a tenuous friendship at best. One time, after the usual order, Angelo approached the table and told Augusto he wanted him to do some gardening for him. Augusto, knowing Angelo extremely well, said, "I'm a-too expensive a-for you, and you a-too a-cheap for a-me." He went on to claim that gardening was an

THE NEW AMERICANS

Italian art and that the work was done with a mystical "touch" that you either had or didn't have and couldn't be learned. It was a gut feeling of knowing the natural techniques of placement of plants in the right perspective and order with the correct combinations of color and hue. This was an instinct, not to be wasted on those who didn't want to spend the money or who were unappreciative. Gardening was not just a job, but also a vocation, a true calling like teaching or the ministry; Augusto selected who was worthy of having the Palazzi name on their work. The extensive pride and meticulous techniques he used in his work could only be those of a man who felt his inferiority in American life and needed to find a niche for acceptance. By his elderly years, he finally had achieved both acceptance and contentment in his life.

Augusto spent his remaining years laboring in his business and, when finished, sitting on his porch or the front steps of his son's Dunmore garden center, holding court to the numerous customers who asked him a great variety of gardening questions. He always strongly recommended peat moss for most things, calling it "gardener's gold." He instructed clients about composting and improving the soil with lots of kitchen scraps and organic wastes. People who had insect problems on roses or ornamentals——he told them to slightly wet the leaves and sprinkle tobacco dust or wood ash on them. For those with yellowing leaves or a dying plant, his old-fashioned biostimulant was a vile-smelling liquid tonic made in an old tub of water with cow, pig, pigeon, or sheep manure mixed in. This was stirred and allowed to ferment for a while, then poured on. It worked like a miracle, quickly reviving the ill plant. Augusto's organic gardening techniques were from his peasant childhood and unique in the age of DDT and Chlordane. He would always refer flower questions to his zinnia bed near Grove Street. He'd walk down to it and show off the massive three-foot tall state fair zinnias. He'd explain how the soil mix was almost all peat moss and cow manure, and how he used his weekly bio-stimulant mix of manure and water to get such great results. The business always sold a lot of manure of all types. At this point in his life, Augusto finally attained the status and self-esteem that had so long eluded him. His expertise was greatly valued, beyond that of his sons or grandsons.

In 1962, at the age of seventy-eight, he began to complain of stomach pain. Everyone urged him to see a doctor, but he had never been to one before and had never been in a hospital. His children had all been born at home, so he had never been in any health care facility for treatment, only to visit sick friends. He was always complaining about the pain. On one Sunday Augusto was especially vociferous, saying the pain would kill him. Bernie, echoing the numerous entreaties to see a doctor, then quipped, "Just tell us where you keep all your money before you die." All his sons developed completely different personality traits than he had, but his work ethic, dedication to perfection, and determination to succeed were ones they all acquired. Augusto was constantly upset about his *"male stomaco,"* and finally in August 1964, the pain was so intense that he was rushed to the hospital. Tests were immediately performed, and doctors decided on emergency stomach surgery. When they opened him up, they discovered his entire lower abdomen was full of cancer and beyond the limited treatment of the day. There was no hope for him. It looked as though it had started in his bladder and had spread rapidly. Perhaps he had gotten this from his younger days when he had labored in the foundry, as he was a non-smoker and metal workers are highly susceptible to this type of melanoma. In his last few days and hours he was delusional, complaining of his mother's early death and abandonment, his father's difficult life and demise, the poverty of his youth, and other family problems. He died in September of 1964.

Of all the author's ancestors, Augusto Palazzi (Palazzini) came from the most difficult and desperate circumstances. He faced extreme poverty in his youth, the early death of his mother, father, and then both brothers. He was rejected in love and went through a failed first marriage to a woman who was an adulteress and deserted him with their children. These events affected him greatly, giving him a dour personality and a general sullen disposition. However, he did raise three fine sons and built a prosperous middle-class business. His personality forced him to show his affection in different ways.

THE NEW AMERICANS

My maternal great grandparents Attilio "chief" Ceccoli and his wife Maria Bianca Ceccoli circa 1930.

LOUIS PALAZZI

Augusto Palazzi, Rose Uguccioni Palazzi, Lou Palazzi Sr., Alcida Foglietta Palazzi, Rose Ceccoli Foglietta, Amedeo Dominick Foglietta

Bob Payton (Uncle of New Orleans Saints Coach Sean Payton), Bob Perugini, Tom Silvano, Bernard "Bernie" "Bruno" Palazzi (Youngest Son), Lou Palazzi Sr., Alcida Foglietta Palazzi, Leonarda Foglietta Sallusti, Mary Boland Gunning, Frank Sallusti

Home of Amedeo and Rose Foglietta (700 SW Webster Ave Scranton, PA)

Arpino Dominick Foglietta (Father of Amedeo Foglietta)

Lucia Maria DeBlasio (Mother of Amedeo Foglietta)

LOUIS PALAZZI

Leonarda Foglietta Sallusti and Alcida Foglietta Palazzi

Leonarda Foglietta Sallusti and Alcida Foglietta Palazzi

THE NEW AMERICANS

The oldest family photo taken in 1871 in Fano, Italy, Marche Province on family farm.

From Left to Right are:
Virginia Ricci Uguccioni (Mother of Rose Uguccioni), Virginia's brother Renato, Renato's wife Beatrice, Mrs. Ricci holding Renato and Beatrice's baby, Mr. Ricci (manager of a large farm), Virginia's sister Beatrice (who never married).

The baby in the photo died in 1984 at the age of 94. Virginia lived in Dunmore from 1921-1941 with Rose and went back to Italy to die.

Part VII

Rose and Tom

Rose Uguccioni (Tomassoni) Palazzi was born on April 9, 1891, in Fano, Italy. She was the sixth surviving child out of thirteen of Fortunato and Virginia Ricci Uguccioni. Her family had been in the region as long as anyone could remember. Her mother's family had managed the estate of a noble and had been relatively wealthy. Her father's family had inherited a small farm of about three acres next to a stream in Fano. The land was silt-based and rich with manure and organic matter. This bottomland soil had a great amount of fertility, and the nearby stream provided ample water for irrigation. The land produced bountiful amounts of vegetables and even semolina wheat. The homestead was large (for those times), constructed of stone with a dirt floor. To provide extra income, both ends of the home were rented to two separate families who huddled in their corners trying to survive in very crowded circumstances. They were kept apart from the large, boisterous Uguccioni family only by a curtain. Living conditions were very cramped.

The Uguccioni family also had the added luxuries of a few farm animals and a "barn." The animal house was the size of most American twelve-foot by twelve-foot sheds today. These things combined with the fertile soil made life livable, but not much more. The extremely large family, the other two in-house families, and the conduct of the father, Fortunato, made life hard. Very little real opportunity existed. Rose's mother, Virginia, was an extremely small woman, even though both her parents were large. Rose's father, Fortunato, was a very big man, being five feet, six inches tall and very heavily built, which was an ancient Uguccioni family trait. Rose inherited her father's height and robust size, but not his deplorable personal idiosyncrasies. He was a person who drank heavily and used frequent physical punishment and abuse on his children. His wife was a shy woman who attempted to protect the children from him, but without much success. Fortunato forced all of the children, as soon as they could walk, to labor in the field and garden next to the home while he made wine and drank. At times he would work outside the home since he was considered the finest butcher in Fano, another Uguccioni trait. His children all learned to be expert gardeners, as well as expert butchers of all types of domestic and wild animals.

Fortunato practiced his trade all over the city, most of the time completely inebriated. He carried his extremely sharp rendering knives to all jobs and could render a hog in less than an hour. Demand for his skills was great, but he came home with little money. Everyone knew he could be paid with wine, and most times he staggered home, completely *"umbriago"* (in the shade), drunk. His neighbors could hear his approach by his loud, bawdy, inebriated ballads, and many times he would fall near their residences. His wife would hide the children and herself, because he was a violent drunk who would beat the kids for the smallest infraction and then force his wife to have sex. The people on the street would always say when he passed, "Hey, Fortunato, in nine months will there be another Uguccioni baby?" He always would tell them he was going home drunk to make sure he had sex with his wife, and there would definitely be another Uguccioni. One time, when he returned, he demanded to eat first. The family sat down to eat pasta; when they did, they discovered the noodles were very uneven and poorly cut. Virginia and her oldest daughter, Regina, explained that Rose had made it for the first time. The remaining siblings laughed at her efforts, and her father hit her. Her mother physically intervened and stated that after all, it was her first time. He then calmed down and ate. Rose soon became an expert maker of all types of macaroni.

Rose began school in kindergarten and excelled in all subjects. She became the best student in her class, and by the third grade, was far above her class peers. She had a great relationship with her teacher, who gave her solid comfort from her tumultuous home life. She loved school, but her education was financially supported by her parents, not general local tax revenue. At the end of the third grade, her drunken father came to school and told her and the teacher that he was withdrawing her and not paying for any more education for a female. He said she could do math and read and write, and that was all she needed as a peasant girl. Her teacher protested vigorously, but to no avail. Rose, in tears and protesting, was hit and dragged home by her father. She made a vow that day that as soon as she could, she would leave home and never return. In her old age, in 1984, Rose recalled how she had no respect or love for her father, and that she never said a prayer for him when he died in 1933 or anytime after that.

Rose and her siblings lived in an abusive environment until each was old enough to leave. In 1905, Riccardo, (Enrico) Secondo, and Dominick, all young men, left for America. Later, all but Regina and Remiggio would go to the New World. At first Rose decided to try to get married and live in Fano. In 1908, Augusto Palazzi, age twenty-three, asked the fourteen-year-old Rose for her hand in marriage. Since she was very young, and he really had nothing to offer her but the same type of miserable peasant lifestyle, she rejected him, and he left for America. The next year and a half, she was courted by Giuseppe Tomassoni, a man in his mid-twenties. He was from a middle-class family of fish merchants. They married in 1910, and Rose was soon pregnant with their first child. She and Giuseppe moved in with his parents in their spacious stone home in Fano. This was a welcome relief for her to finally get out of her parents' homestead. She was required by her in-laws to cook, clean, and do any requested tasks. This she did without complaining since it got her out of her childhood home. She also accepted the role because it was understood that she was of a lower social status and was expected by custom to perform duties for those above her. While she was pregnant, Rose and her husband attended a concert in the park in Fano. She saw and heard a great tenor named Silvano sing Italian love songs and decided to name the child Silvano, if it was a boy. The man was both handsome and musical and caught her fancy, so when she gave birth in 1910, she named her boy Silvano.

Rose's life with Giuseppe mirrored, in many ways, her earlier life at home with her father. Giuseppe and his brothers would load their wagons early in the morning with fresh fish and then take their carts inland to sell to the local farmers in the Fanese campagna. Sometimes they traded for other goods such as wheat, flour, or wine, but most of the time they got paid cash and made a good living. Many times Silvano would accompany his doting uncles, enjoying the ride and the affection they gave him since they were all bachelors with no children. His father, when work was completed in early afternoon, would begin drinking. Rose was again confronted with alcoholism, but her husband's inebriation was different. He was only verbally abusive to her, not physically the way her father had been. This situation was markedly better, but still not what she had hoped life would be or what she had envisioned.

In 1911, Rose got a job as a lifeguard on the beaches of Fano. Because she was a large, athletic, powerful woman who was an excellent swimmer, the vocation fit her perfectly. Many times she pulled distressed swimmers from the surf, and she loved the job. She hoped the extra income could someday be used to move out of the Tomassoni household and buy a home of their own. Her husband preferred living and staying with his parents. Rose continued to work at the beach in the morning, and in the afternoon and evening, she would come home and cook and clean for the entire Tomassoni family. Even though he had plenty of money, her husband refused to move out and buy a home for them. As the years went on, Rose began to loathe the relationship she had with the Tomassonis. Her husband's drinking increased, and her in-laws continued to increase the workload.

In 1915 when Italy entered World War I, Giuseppe joined the Italian Navy to avoid being drafted. His younger brothers managed to escape conscription and continued to work in the business. Giuseppe's time in the Navy was uneventful except for the fact that in late 1916, he contracted the Spanish flu. In early 1917, he died in this worldwide epidemic. This now put Rose and her seven-year-old son in a very difficult situation. She absolutely refused to return to her parent's crowded and abusive homestead, even though most had left, and her parents had gone to America. She did not want to go back to the place of so many bad memories. Life with the Tomassonis was barely tolerable, but since she really enjoyed her job as a lifeguard, she decided to stay with them for a time.

When home from school and on weekends, Silvano accompanied his young uncles on their daily fish routine. He was treated extremely well and was the center of their doting attention. One day, while visiting a farmer to sell fish, his curiosity took him over to a mechanical reaper, and he stuck his right hand in to see how it worked. The blades turned and severed his right index finger. The finger was retrieved, and Silvano was rushed to a local surgeon who reattached it. He told Rose that it probably would turn black and have to be removed. The doctor said the only good thing was that they got it to him quickly, and there was a slight possibility it might heal. He instructed them to watch it closely for three days; if at the end of that time it still were not black, it would probably be healed. Three days went by, and the finger miraculously reattached itself, but it remained hard and dead for the rest of his life. Much later, it became a useful discipline tool: Silvano used it to great effect at Dunmore High School when he was dean of students in charge of discipline.

After Giuseppe's death, life for Rose and Silvano in the Tomassoni household became increasingly difficult. Rose's in-laws continued to demand more work, hoping she would leave and allow them to have Silvano. Because she was so physically strong, coupled with a disciplined and determined personality, she was able to match their requests. In 1918, another problem arose. Giuseppe's youngest brother, about eighteen to twenty years old and a heavy drinker, began to demand sexual favors from Rose in return for her staying with them. She continually fought off his advances, but he persisted, especially when soused. By 1919, her in-laws and her youngest brother-in-law had made the situation intolerable. She wrote to her brothers in America and told both Secondo and Naldo that she had booked passage for both Silvano and herself. Her mother and father and the entire Uguccioni family, except Remiggio and Regina had already left Fano and were in America. She was the last member to immigrate. She did not tell any of the Tomassonis her plans, but her mother-in-law found the full steamer trunk, and in a change of heart, said she would help her leave. She had seen the attempted advances by her youngest son and the scorn and hatred of her husband and other son towards Rose. She finally felt enough compassion to help her. After midnight one night in July 1919, Rose and Silvano, with the help of her mother-in-law, sneaked out of their house and began their trek to America. All ties to the Tomassoni family were ended. On her and Silvano's numerous returns to Italy, later in life, they never encountered any of them again. The final insult from the Tomassonis came in 1962 when they had the audacity to send Rose and Silvano an Italian certified legal document that effectively dispossessed them of their right to any claim on any Tomassoni property. They both were upset and angry, but decided not to seek any legal redress, believing it was not worth the fight.

    Rose and Silvano's trek to the New World began in Genoa in steerage bound for Sicily, to fill up the ship with Southerners. Arriving in Palermo, Rose found the date for embarkation was the following day. The ship was loaded fully and greatly overcrowded. In late summer and early fall of 1919, the harbor of Palermo had to be cleared of the mud that always gathered. A channel was dredged, and a path clearly marked. This was in effect until the next spring when the mud would dissipate. Buoys on each side of the path showed captains which way to steer the ship. In late July of 1919, as the ship was departing, three women were called up to the captain's quarters. The other passengers and crew were puzzled by this. As the ship continued to plow forward, it veered off to the left and got stuck in the mud outside of the markers. All efforts to free it failed. Some crew members came down to explain what happened. They informed the passengers that they would be boarding smaller craft

THE NEW AMERICANS

to take them back to Palermo. The crew was chuckling hysterically while giving these orders. One of them let it slip out that the captain had apparently traded free passage for sexual favors from some female passengers and was so enthusiastic about this that he couldn't wait to get out of port to collect his debt. He wanted the first three immediately. Having three naked women in his cabin distracted him from giving proper steering directions, and the ship went into the mud. The ship's company thought it comical, but to desperate immigrants seeking a better life, it meant an unneeded delay in their dreams and plans. The hiatus in Palermo was over three months. Rose used all of her money supporting both of them. The Italian Navy had only a few ships suitable for the rough waters of the North Atlantic; most were better for the calmer waters of the South Atlantic, heading for Argentina. Finally, the ship *Duc D'Aosta* arrived, and they left for the U.S. Rose had to peel potatoes on the voyage over and work in the kitchen to pay for the remainder of the passage and to get free food for both of them. She hated the trip and despised going up on deck. Silvano loved the pitching and tossing of the ship and enjoyed going up on the top. He became a favorite of the sailors, who constantly had to bring him back down as Rose couldn't bring herself to go up on deck. They arrived at Ellis Island on March 27, 1920, and were picked up by her brother Naldo who rented a butcher shop and grocery store at 306 Broadway Avenue in Scranton. Naldo had been in the USA since 1909 and had been given the choice in 1917 of being deported or joining the U.S. Army fighting in World War I. He chose to join, served, and was discharged a citizen.

Rose's first impressions of Scranton were not favorable. She thought she had arrived in hell. The thick factory smoke from anthracite coal, the dirty homes, the pitch-black, staggering, loud, drunken miners who wandered up and down the street at all hours—these were a stark contrast to the blue sky and pure green water of Fano with its neat homes and clean ocean air. In time, she adjusted to this new life. She and Silvano remained with Naldo only a few months.

Later in the year, they made a trip to visit their brother Enrico in New London, Connecticut. While there, Rose again met Augusto Palazzi, who was renting a room from Enrico. With a great amount of interference, matchmaking, and pushing by her brothers, Rose and Augusto were soon married. Her pestering brothers were happy because they were now relieved of the burden of supporting her and her son. Silvano initially had a difficult time adjusting to his new stepfather, "Palazzin" (Augusto's nickname in the Marchegian section of New London), because he competed for his mother's attention. Finally after a few gifts, especially the horse cart, the stepfather/stepson relationship was solidified.

In June of 1921, Rose gave birth to her second son, Luigi, at their home in Groton, Connecticut. Soon after, they decided to move to Dunmore, Pennsylvania, where Augusto began his gardening business and Rose initially was a housewife. By 1925, the new residence on Blakely Street was completed, and they moved there from their rented apartment on Apple Street. Rose then began the first of many business enterprises over the course of her long life by opening a grocery store. She always said she had a decent life in Italy, and that she came to America to work hard and die rich. She also said that if she had been born a man, she would've died a millionaire. She did eventually accomplish her goals.

In the 1930s, during the Great Depression, Rose closed the store and opened a restaurant called "The Gridiron" in honor of the football prowess of her sons. This was an extremely risky venture as the nation was in dire economic straits. Her persistence, hard work, and determination made her eatery a great success. Like others in Dunmore at the time——the Hawks in candy, the Denaples in garbage and auto parts, and the Gentiles in oil——Rose's nascent enterprise eventually made her wealthy. Her homemade pasta, sauce, and meatballs were known throughout the region. Her red fish ragu from Fano was legendary. In two areas she excelled completely. The first was the special meat/spinach ravioli from the Marches. The second was the roast chicken in the oven, "al forno." Most patrons did not order from the menu, but just asked what she was presently cooking and simply had that. Some would order something different, and she would come out and tell them that wasn't good today and that they really wanted what she was cooking; she would completely change their minds. Her sons used to tell her that she wasted money printing up menus since no one ever used them anyway. The restaurant and bar were always crowded. The miners, coming off shifts, would first pour into the bar to drink and then order something to eat. Other nights they would come in clean, well-dressed, and with their families to dine in the restaurant, which attracted all types of people from various stations in life. The Gridiron was a great success despite the fact that there were five other Italian restaurants within a short distance. All of them did extremely well.

Rose, much to the chagrin of her serious, conservative husband, branched out into many other areas of business. She saw possibilities and opportunities to make money that native-born Americans and people of other ethnicities could not fathom. The profits from The Gridiron were plowed into other ventures. When her husband decided to reduce the size of the garden center, Rose opened a gas station on the site. Across the street, the Hudson Coal Company's store, a very big building, had gone bankrupt along with the parent company. It sat idle for over three years. Rose went alone to the bank president that owned the building and proposed a business arrangement with him. She met with him directly and negotiated the sale of the edifice at almost one-half of the advertised price. She then had the audacity to tell him that he was going to give her a mortgage and a construction loan for the needed renovations at an interest rate below what was listed since the property was in such bad shape. He was completely flabbergasted, but agreed to her terms since he wanted to unload the old store. As she was leaving, he finally got the courage to ask her what she was going to do with the white elephant, assuming she was planning to expand The Gridiron. Rose smiled, said that was correct and left. However, she did not do that, but rather converted the building into eight apartments, all providing monthly income. When Augusto came home from work and found what she had done, he lost his temper and told her she would bankrupt them and put them all in the poorhouse with all her business deals. In a short while, he slowly began to help her renovate the building and landscape the grounds. Eventually, he even moved his smaller nursery to the yard near the apartment house. It became another one of her profitable enterprises.

The addition of another son, Bruno (Bernie), in 1925, completed the family. Even though Rose and Augusto wanted more children, she never became pregnant again. Throughout the twenties and thirties, the family fortunes grew with the constant additions to the family residence/business and the purchase of pieces of land for future use. Rose used to say that land was the best investment because, "Land-a she goes-a up and land-a she-a goes-a down, but-a she always-a has-a value because-a they no make-a any more-a land." Her other investments all did well, but she was especially interested in owning land. She did this, she explained, because of her difficult childhood on a small piece of ground in Fano. Little did she realize that she had accumulated vastly more wealth and property than her parents or ancestors had ever dreamed possible.

Silvano's adjustment to life in America went very well. He quickly picked up the English language and did exceedingly well academically in school. His strong physique and muscular build coupled with his parents' demanding work ethic also made him a tough, physical athlete whom no one picked on in school. He was placed in the third grade in the Dunmore schools. His first teacher, Miss Duffy, had a difficult time pronouncing his Italian name, Silvano Tomassoni. She decided, against his wish and his parents', to call him Tom Silvano, saying it was much easier for her and the other students to pronounce. She also told them it was a more "American" sounding name than his old one. Since they were all trying desperately to fit in, they reluctantly accepted this abbreviated version. His name remained this for the rest of his long life.

In 1924, while a freshman in high school, Tom decided to join the football team. This action began a long association between the family and American football. Tom had been a nationally ranked youth soccer player in Italy when he had left at the age of seven. He thought American football was a type of the European sport. He soon found out that it was completely different. Being an extremely physical athlete, he loved the game more than soccer since he said he now could hit someone and run him or her over without getting penalized. Both parents viewed the game as being strange and violent and vociferously opposed his joining the team. Coach Duffy had heard of Tom's athletic prowess and had seen it in his gym class. He actively recruited him, but had to make a trip to the homestead to convince both parents to let the boy play. With great reluctance, they finally agreed. Duffy decided to try him as both a running and blocking fullback in his single-wing offense. Tom became an immediate starter and beat out much older kids in that position. He quickly became known as the "submarine fullback" because of his low, hard running style. He had four stellar years as a football player in Northeast Pennsylvania.

After his senior season in 1928, many large colleges recruited Tom for football. He narrowed his choices to Penn State and Notre Dame. Knute Rockne, the great Notre Dame coach, made a personal visit to the homestead to convince him to go to South Bend. This personal touch was enough to get him there.

In the fall of 1928, Tom attended Notre Dame and was converted to a running (pulling) guard. He lettered in football and played a lot, but was extremely homesick. A back injury plus the personal visits of the Dunmore superintendent, James Gilleran, a PSU alumnus, convinced him to return home and try Penn State. Tom, however, decided to take a year off and work in the family gardening business.

After a year of personally working with Augusto every day, Tom asked both parents if he could return to college. Augusto was the toughest to convince, but then both finally agreed to let him go as long as he remained there and graduated. This was their only condition. He agreed, was given a football scholarship by Coach Bob Higgins, and spent three stellar years playing at Penn State. He set many records for the Lions and graduated with a degree in physical education in 1933.

Tom considered becoming a professional football player, but decided to take a teaching and coaching position at Dunmore when

LOUIS PALAZZI

Superintendent Gillgallon offered it to him. He became an assistant coach under Duffy and soon after under the legendary James V. Gatto. As an assistant coach he also became one of the coaches of his two younger brothers, Lou and Bernie.

Upon Gatto's retirement in 1944, Tom was named head football coach at Dunmore. The locals, especially the neighbors, complained that the Palazzi family was once again playing politics because Tom first got a teaching job and then became head coach. They sincerely believed this because the following evening after Tom's appointment, the entire school board had a large dinner with a lot of drinks at The Gridiron. When Rose heard these accusations, she became very upset and pointedly told every patron that came into the restaurant from Dunmore that the board of education and superintendent had paid for the meal; no shenanigans took place in either food or monetary form. She even pulled out the invoice for those who had the gall to question her word. Rose was extremely proud of her son and wanted everyone to know that he got the job on merit. Most elderly people in Dunmore today give a lot of credit to the modern football players at the school, but all agree that the two best old-timers who ever played there were Tom Silvano and Fritz Davidson.

During the next ten years, Tom married Ann Sandone and had two children, Barbara and Tommy. He also took classes and got his master's degree in administration. In the early 1960s Tom was made dean of students in charge of discipline at Dunmore High School. He used both his legendary dead finger and the paddle to enforce good behavior. He retired in 1974 and built his dream home on Swartz Street in Dunmore. He really enjoyed his retirement years, living a very long, healthy life.

Rose's mother, Virginia, had come to live with them in the early 1920s. She stayed with them until 1939 when she had saved up enough money to return to Italy. By staying with them, she escaped the abuse of her husband in Eynon, Pennsylvania, and contributed to the restaurant business. She wanted to return to Fano in her old age to die and had saved money to do this. She died there in 1941. Also in that year, Rose and family, protesting strongly, dutifully

THE NEW AMERICANS

followed her husband Augusto to New London, Connecticut. They only stayed a year, then came back home. They watched their three boys grow up, play football, attend and graduate from college, and then get married. Lou and Bernie both served in the military in World War II. After the war, Lou played football for the New York Giants and then began a stellar career as an NFL official for thirty years. He officiated numerous championships, including the 1958 "Greatest Game Ever Played" and Super Bowls IV, VII, and XI. By the late 1940s, Rose and Augusto had become financially secure; they returned to Fano for the first time in 1949. They then made repeated return trips, the last one being in 1963. Rose planned on making more voyages back after Augusto's death in 1964, but always canceled at the last minute. Her last time was with her husband in 1964.

    Rose always made a lot of individual trips to New York City. When business was booming and the demands on her were too great, she would say she had had enough of all of her family and simply leave. Her family knew the taxi she took was to the train station in Scranton, and she would spend a long weekend alone in New York City. On Monday night, she would call her children and say she was at the station. They'd drive down to get her, and she always bought gifts for the grandchildren. She never seemed to remember what she had been mad about in the first place when she came back. This usually happened every two or three months. In 1959, Rose decided to give her restaurant business to her sons. Tom was teaching, coaching, and operating his own diner part-time on route 507 on Lake Wallenpaupack. It was called the Penn Stater, and he ran it on weekends and during the summer months. Lou had recently resigned from teaching/coaching at West Scranton High and was selling Hickok belts and clothes. He only did this for a short time and then began his own gardening/landscaping business. He also continued his NFL officiating career. It fell upon Bernie, the youngest, to take the business over. After World War II, Bernie had worked there primarily as a bartender; after Rose retired, he assumed full responsibility of the operation. He and his wife Vivian continued to make the business prosper, but the long hours, the advent of TV in the homes (the bar had had the only TV for five blocks for almost eight years!) and having very young children took its toll. Rose was extremely disappointed that none of her sons would take over such a good enterprise. Bernie worked for a short time for the Globe Store, then a sporting goods store in downtown Scranton, and then joined Lou in managing his large Clarks Summit store and nursery. The old Gridiron returned to its original function of being a garden center until 1987 when Lou, Sr. moved it one final time to the rear.

Rose and Augusto made their final return to Italy in 1963. Later plans were always put on hold or canceled even though numerous cousins came to the U.S. and invited them back. It seemed fitting that in the year before her husband's death, Rose made a final trip with him to their ancestral homeland. When he did die in 1964, she had little realization of how much longer she would outlive him. Her life after her husband's death centered on her grandchildren. In her eighties (during the 1970s), she mainly lived alone behind her son's garden center. Rose knitted, cooked, and completely enjoyed visitors from Europe and relatives from America. She especially loved cooking everything from scratch; the ingredients were

always fresh. She had her children take her to the local farmers' market to buy the most recent produce; then she would call to have them pick her up. She drove herself until the late 1970s before she began to rely on her grandchildren. It seemed as though Rose constantly managed to bring home two dead chickens, feathers and all, every trip. The family later found out she bought them live and then wrung their necks before carrying them home. She arrived with one in each hand, usually through a crowded store full of gardening customers. Lou, Sr. would shake his head when she arrived, and the curious clients would be very bemused at her trek through their midst. By 1975, the family provided chauffeur service rather than have her drive since she was a terrible operator of a vehicle. On numerous occasions, she had a police escort home because of her unique driving habits. When stopped by law enforcement officials, her standard answer for her erratic driving was, "I don't speak English," even though her language skills were excellent. All local law personnel knew her well and simply took her home. The children would see her coming down the street in her white 1962 Buick Special; as she approached the curb to park, they would grab any stray items nearby so she wouldn't run them over, since she always ended up on top of the curb and sidewalk. They had to take the car from there, backing it carefully into her garage so she could pull out easily.

Rose commanded great respect in the community. At times when customers would give her grandchildren a hard time, she would come out of the backroom and chastise those tough clients. She was especially severe on a Mr. Minora, who always gave everyone trouble. Local animals from the neighborhood also knew her well. She gave them Italian treats, and they all flocked to her when she arrived. Her brother Medardo, who lived next door, had a dog named Buttons (she mispronounced the name as "Butoni") to whom she showed special affection. The animal, in great excitement, would jump and dance when he saw Rose. She would take him inside and give the small Chihuahua leftover pasta and meatballs. When he would eat the meatballs and leave the pasta, she would scold him and physically take him back to finish the noodles. He always obliged her. She knew and saw all the local pets on a regular basis on her walks and across the street in the field. One day she told Lou, Jr. to go across the street to the vacant field and cut some chicory (*cicoria*), a bitter wild green to mix in with the sweeter store-bought lettuce to give their dinner salad a better flavor. When he went over and began cutting, she came out of the house yelling, "*No- no-* don't-a cutta there- go-a down-a more and a-cut. Where you-a cutta, the dogs a-piss-a there." He dumped what he had cut and moved further down.

Rose's mental abilities and skills remained sharp throughout her later years, and she never missed an opportunity to instruct or correct her grandchildren. One day she was asked why she had kept a picture of JFK hanging in her home all these years since he was Irish, and they had not exactly been kind to the family when they had immigrated to Dunmore. She strongly berated her grandson: "Even though you went to college, sometimes you are so dumb.

Don't you realize that I have-a this-a picture hanging because if-a Irishman can-a become-a president, maybe some-a day an Italian will be president?" As usual, she was right. Another time in her home, Rose was knitting and watching a religious show on TV with the volume turned down. It was Rev. Jimmy Swaggart. She then instructed that the sound be turned up. After a time, she asked again for it to be turned down, and so on. This went on a long time, for the entire show. Finally, her grandson asked her what was going on. Rose told him she loved the singing on the religious shows, but hated the constant preaching, and that they were "a too-a busy with-that-a religion." The volume was up for the songs and down for the words. Her outlook on life and family and religion and death was practical and intelligent: the realism of a peasant upbringing coupled with that of a seasoned businesswoman.

At times Rose did come out and help in the store. When she opened the door and the smell of what she was cooking came out, the patrons immediately took notice. At times she would give them pasta or a meatball. For many years she told her children a longtime employee was stealing from them, but they absolutely refused to believe it. Finally, Lou, Sr. caught him red-handed and dismissed him. Rose proved, once again, that even in her elderly condition her faculties were as sharp as ever. She was as hardworking and dedicated to her family in her very old age as she had been as a young woman.

In 1981, on her ninetieth birthday, Rose announced to everyone that she was ready to die. She said when the good Lord was ready, she was willing to go since she felt it was time. She continued to say that she had lived a rich and rewarding life, much greater than anything she had imagined, and it was now time to go. She was not tired of living, but of the constant daily pain from her ailments. She had a very sensitive stomach (which her son Bernie inherited), requiring her to carefully monitor her diet. If she did not watch it closely, she would end up vomiting all that she ate. For breakfast, it was mainly a banana on dry toast with coffee that always had a shot of anisette or sambuca in it. One day she told her grandson to get the sambuca from the bottom of the cabinet for her coffee. He looked and found there was none left and informed her of this. She asked what was left in there, and he told her the only thing was his dad's Canadian whisky. She said, "That's a-okay; it'll work-a just-a as good as-a the anisette." It was her morning stimulant. Lunch and dinner consisted of chicken broth and pastina. She also had terrible arthritis in her extremities, and had suffered a series of TIAs (mini-strokes). Doctors felt she had had at least ten of those by her ninetieth birthday.

When she was ninety-one, Rose and the family got a big surprise. One day they walked back into her apartment and found an elderly man sitting at the kitchen table eating pasta. He spoke no English, only Italian. She informed them he was the same age as she; his name was Pepe, and he had recently arrived from Fano. She went on to say that he had been a boyfriend of hers seventy-five years earlier in the old country and had recently written her about coming to America. She said she had written back inviting him to come and stay with her. The family asked her his last name. She said she didn't remember it and added that he was going to be there a while. Every day he stayed, her grandson's father and uncles would get more nervous about his intentions and what was going on between them. Finally, one day when Pepe was out walking, she told all of them that Pepe had proposed marriage to her. They were all aghast. She said she had turned him down. They asked why. She said she told him she had buried two husbands, did not want to bury a third, and all he could do was eat and create work for her— cooking, cleaning, and doing laundry. She said the biggest reason was that neither one of them was capable of performing sex anymore, and if "You can't-a have-a fun in-a marriage, why get a-married?" Within a few days of being rejected, Pepe left and returned to Fano. They never saw or heard from him again.

After Augusto's death in 1964, Rose kept the home they had purchased in Florida many years before. She continued to go to Florida every winter and stayed in the home for five more years, then sold it. She purchased a time-share efficiency apartment and continued her annual winter trek. She always had numerous visitors at her apartment: her own immediate family, her Uguccioni relatives, and her husband's Palazzi relatives. Her great-niece, Anita Palazzi Moitoza, who had a home in Florida, always made it a point to check on her. Rose would write letters home every week in prose that was half Italian and half English. The family completely and thoroughly enjoyed reading those. She had plenty of company in the winter far from home.

In late December 1984, she called her family from Florida unexpectedly and said she was extremely weak. She said she had just had a stroke. Since they knew about her numerous previous TIAs, they understood it was serious. She also said that this one had been so strong that it would probably kill her. Tom immediately flew to Florida to get her and bring her home. She was put into the Moses Taylor Hospital in Scranton. The day she arrived home, she slipped into a deep coma.

Rose was in a coma almost three months, from January to March of 1985. The doctors suggested they try all types of stimulation to bring her out of it. They all attempted speaking to her, touching her, and in desperation, pleading with her in her native Italian in an effort to revive her from the coma. She only moved her eyes slightly with their last technique. She expired in March of 1985 at ninety-four years old, only a month shy of her ninety-fifth birthday.

Rose left a great legacy to her sons and

grandchildren. She had left ignorance and abuse in Italy; through her intelligence, determination, and especially hard work, she had achieved everything she wanted in life and had expired satisfied and comfortable. Her character and way with people coupled with her acute business sense were examples to everyone who knew her and wanted to emulate her expertise. She faced the same or more discrimination than other ethnic groups encountered, but was able to overcome this and achieve success due to her exemplary qualities. Rose was a great, positive example for all of the family, and if she had been a man, her possibilities would have been endless.

Part VIII

The Other

The exodus of family members from Italy started immediately after Attilio left in the 1890s and continued up to the last ones who arrived in the 1960s. Very few actually remained in the old country, though some who did come, facing extreme prejudice and discrimination, stayed a while and then returned. They did not operate under any clear-cut determination to stay or go, but rather simply to survive by finding employment. This was their driving motive, and it didn't matter whether they were in America or Italy. Some went back and forth numerous times in an attempt to find their place in the world. Their basic instinct was simple survival.

Soon after Attilio arrived, he was first joined by his brother Dante (in 1897), followed by his brother Angelo and sister Giulia. They all lived with him for a time and then began their new lives in different parts of Northeast Pennsylvania. Their descendants and distant cousins all remain there to this present day.

Amedeo only had one family member come to the New World, his baby sister Christine. Her tragic story was previously told. His brother, Pasquale, attempted to come to the U.S. in the 1950s, but could not get in. The restrictive Quota Acts passed in the 1920s were still in effect, and they severely discriminated against Italians.

LOUIS PALAZZI

One final try was made in the 1960s, but his age and the required paperwork made him remain in Italy. The family visited him, his family, and his sisters' families in the 1970s and 1980s.

The Uguccionis continued to flow to America. The entire family (with two exceptions), including the father, Fortunato, and mother, Virginia, came to the U.S. Virginia, having had enough of Fortunato's alcoholism and abuse, came first with her young sons. She even scratched out the name "Uguccioni" on the ship manifest and wrote her maiden name, "Ricci." She moved into her son Medardo's home and spent time between his home and her daughter Rose's across the street. Virginia remained in Dunmore a long time, from her immigration to her return to Italy in 1939. She helped out in Medardo's bakery and Rose's restaurant and slowly saved her money. In 1939, she returned from a shopping trip in downtown Scranton and announced to the family that she was returning to Fano to die. They all laughed at her and asked where she was going to get the money for passage. To their astonishment, she produced a large amount of cash she had gotten from tips over the years— enough for the fare for the trip, and enough to live off for a long time. She left in 1939, never having become an American citizen, and died in Fano in 1941.

Fortunato followed his estranged wife and children to the New World early in the 1900s. The ship manifest that carried him to America listed him as being five foot, seven inches tall, and "very robust." Out of hundreds of passengers on this ship, he was the only one with a comment after his name. He went to Eynon, Pennsylvania, where he lived with his son. He avoided his wife in Dunmore and his other children, but they all did visit him on occasion. He was fifty-five years old when he arrived and was supposed to work as a coal miner. He worked one day in the mines and hated it. Every day, with lunch packed, he would leave the house to work in the mines, but in reality he would walk a block, wait for everyone to leave the home for work, and then return. He would hide in a local park at times, or slip into the basement to avoid going to work. He rubbed coal on his face and clothes, pretending that he had slaved in the pits. The family pressured him to work, but he refused. Finally,

THE NEW AMERICANS

Fortunato began to revert to his old habits in Italy, where he worked as a butcher. People took animals
to his son's home, and he rendered all types of meat. His reputation spread quickly, and he soon had more work than he could handle slaughtering hogs, chickens, and cattle. He made some cash from these services, but also traded his skills for wine. He continued to drink to excess, even at times while butchering, completely inebriated as he had done in Italy. He possessed considerable skill, since he never once cut or injured himself even when drunk, and his work was considered the best in the upper Lackawanna Valley. He spent little time with his wife as she avoided him as much as she could, and he was present only at family gatherings or on holidays. Around 1928, he talked about returning to Fano. Since he felt he was unwanted by his family and his personal habits were not those of the rest of his brethren, his decision was made easier. Fortunato returned to the old homestead in Fano, where he resumed his excessive imbibing and died from alcoholism in 1931. His alcoholism and bad habits fortunately died with him and were not passed down to his progeny.

His older brother Attilio soon followed Augusto's immigration in 1908. Attilio and his wife joined Augusto in New London, Connecticut in 1910. They both had an extremely difficult time existing in Fano even though they resided with Attilio's father, Luigi. He also took an "immigrant job" as an iron molder, like Augusto. Augusto and Albina resumed their bitter hatred for each other, and in a very short time, she returned to Italy. Albina despised the U.S. because of the prejudice, discrimination, and daily ethnic slurs that she encountered in New London. She constantly wrote letters to Attilio, badgering him to return. Finally, he did, later in the year. However, soon after his return, he spent all of his savings and was unable to find work. In 1912, he rejoined Augusto in New London and went back to fabricating metals. He stayed almost two years. Due to his wife's pestering and urging, he went back again in 1914. Augusto warned him about returning due to the impending war in Europe, but he did not heed his younger brother's advice and returned. Augusto cursed his sister-in-law Albina and forbade any contact with Attilio's family. He never spoke of him again, saying for the rest of life he had only one brother, Massimo.

Attilio's existence remained unknown to the author's family until recently. Attilio had a very difficult time finding work on his return to Italy. In 1915, when Italy joined the Allies in World War I, he was recruited by the Italian army. Having few employment prospects, he joined. He quickly, at age thirty-four, became a member of Italy's elite soldiers, the Bersaglieri. Attilio's desperate act in becoming a soldier did result in his finally being able to support his family. He saw combat and was probably wounded at the huge battle of Caporetto against the Austrian/German armies. He was then captured with large numbers of other Italians. Attilio remained in an Austrian POW camp at Kleinmunchen, Austria, and died there from his wounds in 1921. This was long after other Italian POWs had been repatriated to Italy. Honoring Augusto's wishes, there was never any contact between the two brothers' descendants until November 2002.

Almost all of Augusto's nieces and nephews eventually made it to North America. The first to immigrate was Nina Palazzi, oldest daughter of Massimo. She married a widower, Amedeo Alegi, and settled in Taunton, Massachusetts in the early 1900s. When Massimo died in 1917, his oldest son, Ugo, tried to help his family by working in the brickyard, but soon realized he would have to leave. He went to Taunton in 1921 and lived with Nina and Amedeo for a long time. In the early 1930s, he married Idea Alegi, Amedeo's daughter from his first wife, who had died. He and his new bride honeymooned in Dunmore with his Uncle Augusto and Aunt Rose. They then settled in Taunton, and both Nina's and Ugo's descendants live there today.

In 1954, Augusto's other nephew, Federico Palazzi, and his family immigrated to North America. Augusto had visited them in three trips to Italy from 1954 to 1956 and had attempted to arrange transport and immigration to Dunmore. Again because of the Quota Acts, he was unable to do this. Even though blood relatives of those in the U.S. got preference, it was still difficult to get them to the States because of the discriminatory nature of the

THE NEW AMERICANS

laws. The family could not be brought to Dunmore, so they followed other Fanese and Marchigiani to Windsor, Ontario, Canada, where Federico worked in construction. His eldest son became a college-educated accountant and an accomplished musician, while his younger sons established one of the biggest tile, marble, granite, and rug businesses in North America in Windsor.

In 1959, Luisa Palazzi Pascucci, the youngest daughter of Massimo Palazzi, also immigrated to Windsor. She and her family had moved into the Federico household in Fano when they had left for North America in 1954. Five years later, they also immigrated. Like their cousins in Windsor, they also entered the tile and marble business.

The last known relatives of Augusto's who immigrated to North America were Fernando Palazzi and his wife, Brunella. They also settled in Windsor. He was Attilio's grandson. There were supposedly many others from the Attilio branch who made it to Windsor, but purportedly they had legal problems (civil and criminal), and were either jailed or deported. Since relations and discussions were never good between the Augusto/Massimo branches and the Attilio branch, little is actually known. In the Augusto branch itself, there was only one modern contact between the Libero (first family) branch and the second family. This was a brief contact in the year 2002. Efforts were made to re-establish contact with the first family of Augusto, but they did not lead to either meetings or further information.

Part IX

The Legacy

Louis J. Palazzi, Jr.'s family's exodus from Italy, which began during the Revolutionary War, became a flood in the late 1800s. By the 1960s, very few known blood relatives actually remained in the old country. Most were his maternal grandfather Amedeo's relatives in Civatella Casanova in Abruzzo. There were a few Ceccolis near Foligno, a few direct and many distant Uguccionis in Fano, and almost no direct Palazzi or Palazzini in the Marches. Their leaving was not a planned, detailed attempt to improve their lives, but rather a desperate measure for survival. They all seemed to adjust their goals and ambitions as they made their way in a slow, deliberate process in the New World. Like all American immigrants, they faced immediate prejudice and discrimination; it was possibly the worst for Italians, and they took employment in the vocations that no other Americans would accept. However, in a short time, they realized that America offered them two things of unique and great advantage not available in the Old World. The first was unlimited opportunity. Where most immigrant families found the mines, sweatshops, or mills, Louis's family, with no education or training, discovered the immense benefits of the American free enterprise system. Almost all became entrepreneurs. At a young age, they were all instructed how they could achieve and have anything they wanted if they were willing to work hard. Comparisons were constantly made between the U.S. and the Old World and how the opportunities here were endless. The earlier immigrants who settled in Dunmore and their descendants in the neighborhood considered Louis's family pushy, aggressive, and driven. They had difficulty understanding why they hadn't taken the usual path of factories, mines, or mills the way they, at that time, were doing. Louis's grandparents, with the different attitude and perspective of newcomers, saw things that native-born Americans could not. Their myopia was his ancestors' vision. Every enterprise and business they started succeeded magnificently, not because of extensive entrepreneur training, but because of determination, perseverance, and hard work. This was their greatest legacy.

The second difference between America and Europe was educational opportunities. All of his grandparents were amazed at the fact that education in America was free. They were more surprised to discover that it was all-encompassing, up to the twelfth grade. The other oddity for them was that it included people of all social classes, ethnic origins, and levels of income. Since their rudimentary schooling had been in costly parochial academies in Italy, the American system was an incredible asset to their children who aspired to achieve equality with other Americans. They quickly realized this was the avenue for Americanization, socialization, acceptance, and most important of all, economic advancement. All of their children became high school graduates, tripling the level of schooling they had received themselves. Beginning with Tom Silvano in 1928, most continued on to get college degrees, with Lou and Tom eventually receiving master's degrees. The college level was extremely difficult for them since they had no money to pay for it, and their language at home was Italian. All their offspring had football scholarships (Tom), or worked their way through (Lou and Bernie), or used the GI Bill of Rights to get their advanced degrees. This educational training enabled their generation to become professionals and businessmen and set a great example for the next. The following generation had the great fortune of having every grandchild become a college graduate.

The author may be contacted at:

Palazzigardening@yahoo.com

www.ingramcontent.com/pod-product-compliance
Lightning Source LLC
Chambersburg PA
CBHW061501040426
42450CB00008B/1448